BILL FARREL

7 SIMPLE SKILLS™ for Every Man

The author is represented by the literary agency of Alive Communications, Inc., 7680 Goddard Street, Ste. #200, Colorado Springs, CO 80920.

Cover by Harvest House Publishers Inc., Eugene, OR

7 SIMPLE SKILLS FOR EVERY MAN

Published by Harvest House Publishers
Eugene, Oregon 97402
www.harvesthousepublishers.com

Library of Congress Cataloging-in-Publication Data
Farrel, Bill, 1959-
7 simple skills for every man / Bill Farrel.
pages cm
ISBN 978-0-7369-5761-8 (pbk.)
ISBN 978-0-7369-5762-5 (eBook)
1. Christian men—Religious life. 2. Christian men—Conduct of life. 3. Life skills. I. Title.
II. Title: Seven simple skills for every man.
BV4528.2.F428 2014
248.8'42—dc23

2014000545

Printed in the United States of America

14 15 16 17 18 19 20 21 22 / BP-JH / 10 9 8 7 6 5 4 3 2 1

Dedicated to Lee Hough,
who was my friend and literary agent
until cancer took him to the presence of
the Eternal Author of Simplicity.
Lee was a faithful defender of what is
right and true in this world and
a true believer in the power of simple skills.

ACKNOWLEDGMENTS

Throughout my life I have been attracted to people who know how to make things simple. My dad had a high-level career as an aerospace engineer, yet he could talk about the science of rockets at a level we could all relate to. My high school football coaches had an uncanny ability to break down and communicate intricate plays so I knew how to respond in the heat of battle. This book is my contribution to the legacy of work shaped by the talented teachers, coaches, and leaders who showed me how most situations can be effectively navigated with a few simple skills. A simple approach to life makes sense to me; after all, the greatest message on earth is the uncomplicated gospel of Jesus Christ that makes eternal life accessible with childlike faith. And, as the greatest teacher in history, Jesus presented the most important principles of life through simple, relatable stories for the average person.

I am forever grateful to Jim Conway for his example of translating well-researched, academically sound relationship principles into easy guidelines ordinary people could follow. I am even more grateful to my wife, Pam, for working hard alongside me to uncover the simple skills that have empowered our personal lives, our love for each other, and our parenting.

I also want to thank Bob Hawkins and the staff at Harvest House Publishers. Bob, you have raised up a dedicated, practical staff of professionals who believe that life's greatest treasures can arrive in simple packaging. I want to especially thank Hope Lyda for her diligent work editing the manuscript. Hope, I admire you for tackling a book for men, and I believe your contributions made this a better book that will help more men discover the simple truths of life.

Finally, I want to acknowledge my Savior, Jesus Christ. Without his investment in my life, I would have made things hopelessly complicated. Thanks for your simple love.

CONTENTS

Introduction
Simple (But Not Easy) Skills to Live By

I take a simple view of living. It is, keep your eyes open and get on with it.

Sir Laurence Olivier

My friend Ken and I were driving on Water Street in St. John's, Newfoundland, which happens to be the oldest road in North America. He was sharing the history of the town and we were marveling at the number of establishments with origins going back to the 1800s. As we passed the intersection of George Street, Ken said, "You probably wouldn't want to be on George Street late on a Saturday night. That is where most of the pubs are."

"It must be kind of like Bourbon Street in New Orleans."

"It may not be quite as crazy as that but it gets pretty wild," Ken said. "They used to have a lot more fights than they do today. As you can imagine, most of the men who left at closing time were pretty drunk. The owners of the pubs noticed that most of the fist-fights started with men getting lippy with each other. They decided to hand out suckers at closing time to every man as he walked out the front door. That simple act stopped about ninety percent of the fights."

I was struck by the lesson in this great story: there are simple solutions to complex problems.

This should not surprise any of us because we experience this truth every day in various ways. We implement simple steps to access complex technology. Few of us understand the complexity of the code that runs our computer, but we casually harness its potential with a power button, a mouse, and a few keystrokes. With a couple of pedals and a steering wheel, we effortlessly direct powerful automobiles. And with the click of a simple icon, we instantly connect with people around the world through social media.

It's Kind of Like Jesus

Life operates this way because it is a reflection of the author of life, Jesus. He was the master of taking complex processes of life and boiling them down to simple principles any man can grasp. Consider:

> "'Love the Lord your God with all your heart and with all your soul and with all your mind'...'Love your neighbor as yourself.' All the Law and the Prophets hang on these two commandments" (Matthew 22:37, 39-40).

> "Not so with you. Instead, whoever wants to become great among you must be your servant, and whoever wants to be first must be slave of all" (Mark 10:43-44).

> "Everyone who calls on the name of the Lord will be saved" (Romans 10:13).

> Husbands, love your wives, just as Christ loved the Church and gave himself up for her (Ephesians 5:25).

Simple Doesn't Mean Easy

We must never confuse simple with easy because life is lived in an arena where we face fierce competition, high stakes, and considerable obstacles. Most days require you to give the best of who you are at the highest level you can operate. At every turn, there are forces that would like nothing better than to run you off the road, ruin your reputation, and rob your willingness to press on.

Yes, life is strenuous and intricate, but it can be navigated with a series of simple skills. These skills should be well-known and frequently followed by most men, but, for whatever reason, they've gotten lost along the way so that most men are unaware of them. The complexity of life has led many people to create complicated solutions that are hard to remember, harder to implement, and nearly impossible to maintain.

In an effort to recover some of the simplicity, we have become too focused on "don't." For fear that we will make a mess of things, we have been told most of our lives:

- Don't be angry.
- Don't hit others.
- Don't make bad decisions.
- Don't be selfish.
- Don't look at that.
- Don't be so loud.
- Don't be so quiet.
- Don't argue with me.
- Don't be so pushy.
- Don't be a sore loser.

The result? We all have a pretty good idea of what we aren't supposed to be!

But a man's life is not supposed to be defined by what he isn't and what he doesn't do. Men are created to act, accomplish, and inspire. We are made

- *strong* so we can overcome obstacles,

- *focused* so we can pursue worthwhile goals,
- *passionate* so we can have an enduring influence on our world.

What a Man Wants

At the time I am writing this book, I have a one-year-old grandson. Without having to teach him, he has a fascination with footballs, basketballs, baseballs, soccer balls—in fact, any kind of ball will do. I took him to visit my son (his dad) at a football practice at the local high school. We walked past the tennis team practicing on the courts. When Rocco heard the "pop" of the first serve, his head snapped around just in time to see the yellow projectile skim along the ground. He squealed loudly, "Ooh!" Every serve received the same enthusiastic response. When the tennis balls from serving practice got stuck in the chain link fence, he danced from ball to ball, touching each sphere and laughing in wonder at the sight.

It won't be long before people start telling him he is being silly. He will be told to calm down, quiet down, and sit down. As a family, we are committed to help him pursue his interests in wise and ambitious ways; but out in the world, he will do that amidst a chorus of don'ts. How many of us have grown up with more restriction than inspiration?

Men are equipped with an innate desire to live productive lives and pursue vital relationships. Every man wants a career that needs what he has to offer, a woman who thinks he is incredible despite his faults, and an adventure to pursue that captivates the passion he carries in his soul. And we want all three of these to be simple enough that we can succeed.

For men, this is a simple pursuit. We think in clear terms of what we want.

- "I want a job I enjoy."

- "I want to be in love with an interesting and interested woman."
- "I want to have good experiences with the people I care about."
- "I want to do things that make me feel like a man."

The world we live in, however, is rugged and unpredictable. Life tends toward the complex and complicated. You will be confronted with a wide range of emotional needs, situational challenges, and unexpected consequences. As things get more complicated, you will notice that your motivation level drops. The complexity creates confusion, which makes you feel weak—and men don't like to feel weak. The more complicated life becomes, the more a man struggles with his motivation to stay interested in his pursuits.

There is good news! There are a few simple skills any man can practice that will enable him to stay on track. Even complicated situations can be navigated with simple abilities that keep men strong, focused, and effective. I will share how these simple skills have helped me in my journey, and I will challenge you to apply these skills to your everyday life.

My goal is that we will all adopt the attitude of the influential British economist E.F. Schumacher, "Any intelligent fool can make things bigger, more complex, and more violent. It takes a touch of genius—and a lot of courage—to move in the opposite direction."

Let's move forward with courage.

CHAPTER 1

Focus Your Passions

A man's desires will inspire dreams or inflict damage.

Every solution to every problem is simple. It's the distance between the two where the mystery lies.

Derek Landy, *Skulduggery Pleasant*

Every man knows that he has strong drives within him that can motivate him and also mess things up. When they are focused on healthy pursuits, these drives bring out the best in us. Conversely, when our passions turn their focus to self-serving lusts, they bring out the worst in us and damage important relationships. The good news is that God created us with passion that will lead us to be effective in our careers, engaged in a loving marriage, courageous in ministry efforts, and bold when making life-improvements for ourselves and others. When our passions are applied skillfully, the results are amazing.

In 2001, Tim Westergren was forty-four and trying to get Pandora Radio established. He was out of money and wondering if he had the skill or vision to make it happen. He and his colleagues thought about cutting their losses, but they had a passion in their hearts. Many people told them they were crazy when fifty of them decided to defer $1.5 million in salaries over a two-year period. Tim even maxed out eleven credit cards before they were rescued by an investment in 2004.[1] Today Pandora boasts 70.9 million active users with monthly revenues exceeding $30 million.[2]

Elon Musk had never been involved in designing anything and had no experience in the aerospace industry when he decided to start SpaceX, a private company dedicated to reducing the cost and increasing the reliability of space missions. He took the risk of pouring in most of the capital from his sale of PayPal (the company he cofounded). In December 2008, SpaceX won a $1.6 billion contract with NASA to resupply the International Space Station, and today its annual revenue is over $100 million.[3]

Michael Chasen became the cofounder of Blackboard at age thirty-six. In an interview featured on Forbes.com, he describes the risk:

> Matthew Pittinsky and I were working in the Higher Education Group at KPMG when we noticed a trend: Schools were spending millions to wire classrooms and dormitories to the Internet, but there was no software to make the investment useful for teaching and learning. We decided to quit our jobs and start our own company to design that software. The biggest risk was telling my fiancé one month before our wedding that I was going to quit my high-paying job to gamble on a "big idea" with my old friend and college roommate—not exactly what she had signed up for. Fortunately, she was very supportive and encouraged me to follow my dream. She also said she would still marry me. Risk averted.[4]

Today Blackboard is an online portal used by thousands of universities as the primary communication tool between faculty and students.

These three men are ordinary in many respects. They are hardworking men who paid attention to the passion that rose up in their hearts. The incredible results have provided opportunities for many others to live out their passions. They are examples of what can happen when a man focuses the passions of his heart in a positive way.

Activating Passions for Good

Saying to men, "Your life will be better if you just turn off your passions," is like saying, "Your car will work better if you turn off the engine." A man without passion is a lifeless, bored individual who feels little, inspires no one, and lacks the drive that causes others to want to follow his example.

Yet we know certain passions, when unchecked, create damage and complicate our lives. Conventional wisdom tries to tame these passions with well-meaning rules. Yet again, we receive a list of don'ts as a weak replacement for real guidance.

- Don't lust.
- Don't be selfish.
- Don't work so hard.
- Don't watch so much television.
- Don't take the second look.
- Don't think about sex.
- Don't get angry.
- Don't drink anymore.

Of course these are good outcomes we are seeking, but the "don't do that" approach is not effective as a strategy. Strong passions require an aggressive approach that recognizes the power of our desires, the potential we possess for doing good with them, and the pervasive distractions in our world. It is not enough to simply avoid behaviors that could harm our health, deteriorate our relationships, and interrupt our ability to succeed. Every man I know has tried this approach only to see his intensity turn into anger, his romantic interest turn into lust or pornography, his influence turn into manipulation, and his appetites turn into overindulgence.

The great struggle for men is to find a way to live strong and get important needs met without resorting to self-destructive habits and attitudes. An effective strategy will include a courageous admission that we relentlessly look for ways to express our passions, and we need the camaraderie of other men to keep these passions focused.

Passions in My Life

I am happy to say that I am a passionate man. In my career, I have an enduring desire to help as many people as possible grow in their most important relationships. I am convinced that the most vital relationship is with Jesus. When an individual comes to grips with the fact that he is a sinner and that Jesus died on the cross to pay the penalty for every mistake, every bad attitude, and every hurtful action, he discovers the greatest hope of his life.

Faith and Family

At the moment a man decides to trust Christ as his Savior, the Holy Spirit takes residence in his heart and adds an ability and power to his life that cannot exist any other way. A supernatural force invades his body and provides opportunities for growth, strength, freedom, and victory that were previously impossible. For this reason, I want everyone I know and everyone I meet to discover this life-changing, life-empowering relationship.

The power of family relationships is also significant and life-shaping. A man and woman who are in love have the ability to greatly influence another. When people observe how a loving couple treats and respects one another, they are often motivated to learn from them and adopt simple convictions and beliefs that become lifelong philosophies.

I am naturally driven to teach others what I have learned about being a husband, father, and grandfather. I gain great satisfaction when others "get it" when it comes to loving their wives and influencing their families in a positive way. And, I am crazy about my kids and grandkids. I am willing to make any commitment, take any risk, and endure any inconvenience to promote growth in their lives and cheer them on in their pursuits.

I've been amazed how willing and eager I have been to work for my family without having to be convinced. The reason is simple: I am passionate about them, so any sacrifice seems justifiable. One dramatic example of this passion in action was during the last week of Pam's third pregnancy. We were just about finished building our home, and I was preparing for the final inspection.

My goal was to get the home completed so we wouldn't have to move more than once with an infant. The days before Caleb was born, I stayed up for seventy-two hours working full-time and tending to final details. The day of the birth was glorious as a new member of our family came into the world. I slept in the hospital that night alongside Pam just in case she needed anything. At about 2:00 a.m., the IV came out of her arm and blood was spurting on the floor. Pam tried to wake me up, but I was comatose. She had to call for a nurse who, upon quick and inaccurate assessment of the scene, had a couple of sarcastic comments to say about the man in the room who was asleep while the women did all the work.

As Pam told her about the previous week, the nurse's demeanor softened. People are inspired by passion applied purposefully to life. When passion is spent selfishly, it attracts criticism and breeds contempt; but when passion comes from a genuine motivation to live well, it is uplifting and influential.

Sex

I am also passionate about having an active, mutually satisfying sex life with my wife. When my sex life is balanced, I am more responsible with work, more reasonable with decisions, more resilient with the obstacles of life, and more relaxed in all areas. For good and bad, men have strong sexual desires and are proud of the fact that they have a quick and significant response to sexual stimulations. It doesn't take much to raise interest and motivate them to perform with great energy and desire. A man's eyesight becomes laser focused to see great beauty in his wife, even when she is feeling her least attractive.

The desire is like a fire sometimes, like a powerful engine at other times, and like a wild animal at others. It is seldom tame and gentle. Left unchecked, it has the potential to consume a man's decisions, get out of control, and create damage. In fact, a man must learn to be romantic and relational in order to direct his passionate power in a productive way. But he welcomes the challenge because a marriage relationship is one of the greatest gifts in a man's life.

Play and Pleasures

In a less important way, I am passionate about my convertible. It is just a VW Cabriolet, but I love driving it, and I love making modifications to it. It is simple enough that I can work on it without having to gain a new education every time I want to fix or change something. It is fast enough to give me a thrill every once in a while. It is agile enough to handle curves at speeds faster than the posted limits—and I can put the top down! The wind that races around me has a mysterious ability to take away stress.

Most of the time, I am able to keep these passions in balance. I plan my schedule so each of these pursuits gets time, focus, and resources. They are passions, however, and don't voluntarily stay in-line with sound reasoning and disciplined living.

Roles We Play

Since we are made in the image of God, we have the ability to be creative. We can create businesses, conceive children, synthesize existing ideas into new ideas, develop raw property into communities, and build a legacy that reaches multiple generations. Unfortunately, many of us also create versions of ourselves to justify engaging in activities that can't be justified by our convictions or common sense. We invent these caricatures of ourselves because we don't know how to meet raw needs in appropriate ways. We, therefore, allow a less mature, more manipulative reflection of ourselves engage in behaviors we disapprove of and then spend enormous amounts of energy trying to hide this persona from the people in our lives. The secrecy strengthens the actor in us.

Each time we get away with one of these behaviors or decisions, we convince ourselves we can cohabit with this harmful friend.

I recently heard Nate Larkin speak at a Promise Keepers Canada event about our ability to create personas that allow us to give a voice to our passions. Every once in a while someone says something that jumps out at me and demands my attention. Nate created one of those moments. The truth was instantly obvious.

Roles in My Life

I, like you, have a number of manifestations of who I am that provide opportunity for my passions. Some of them are very responsible while others are childish and selfish.

Redeemed Bill

I love helping people and tenaciously embracing my call to ministry. Shortly after I discovered the transforming mystery of trusting Christ as my Savior, I began a Bible study with my brother and our high school friends. This is when Redeemed Bill was activated. My desire to study God's Word with others grew into a commitment to a campus ministry during college. I found the work exhilarating and satisfying at a deeper level than anything else I have ever experienced. I can honestly say that ministry feels easier to me than other career pursuits I have been involved in because there is an enduring passion in my soul for teaching the Bible, helping people grow in their faith, supporting churches so they can continue to reach out to others, and putting up with the hassles that go along with ministry work.

I expect people to bring problems with them because we are all imperfect. I am not surprised when churches are inefficient because it is more like a family than a corporation. I honestly believe pastors and church staff members are the most important influence on society, morality, family life, and community development. I am also convinced that the average church attender is the key to all things good in our world. As a result, the stumbles and obstacles that go along with church involvement don't bother Redeemed Bill.

Fortunately, I operate here most of the time.

Responsi-Bill

Another positive manifestation of who I am is Responsi-Bill. This is the persona that keeps my bills paid, does yard work, answers the phone when my kids call, and focuses on my grandkids. Responsi-Bill works hard, keeps promises, makes other people feel important, focuses on deadlines, and does what is right simply because it is right. This is a comfortable persona because my dad was a good role model of a man honoring his word. He was consistently loyal at work. He has been married to my mom for over sixty years. He has a simple philosophy of doing the right thing because it is the right thing. He lacked relational sophistication and he wasn't a big risk-taker, but he was steady, reliable, and dedicated to his principles. Responsi-Bill draws from his influence and finds it relatively easy to commit to hard work and sound principles.

Restless Bill

I find passions in my soul that are not easily addressed by Redeemed Bill or Responsi-Bill. Because of this, Restless Bill is a persona I can fall into when I struggle. For instance, I am prone to feeling lonely. I know a lot of people, but I haven't been good at letting them support me. I grew up in a home that was run by fear, and a lack of trust was instilled in my soul. My mom was convinced that everyone she got to know was out to hurt her. She was vocal about it and insisted on family decisions that preserved our isolation to make her feel more secure.

Restless Bill is not an asset. This is the part of me that is frequently afraid that bad news is right around the corner. I want to open up, but I feel that vulnerability will be misunderstood and manipulated. I manufacture the belief that I must always give to others but will never receive much in return. I also spend significant emotional energy convincing myself that I must meet my own needs because no one will ever care enough to reach out and truly care about what matters to me.

As a result, Restless Bill gives rise to hurt feelings, bouts of silence, and fantasy relationships. I overreact to Pam's evaluations as I accuse them of being criticisms. I sulk around her because I feel powerless to communicate to her what is really important to me. I feel ridiculed by her even though I know she is my biggest fan. I often feel overrun by her in conversation, so I just clam up and silently nurse resentment. I then use the loneliness to justify imaginary relationships.

Most of the time, I create a version of Pam in my mind that is perfectly in tune with my needs and sensitively responsive to them. This version of Pam flirts often, has a lively appetite for sex, and takes a soft approach to interaction. Of course, when this Pam doesn't show up, I pull back in disappointment and justify my feelings of self-pity. At other times, I picture nameless, faceless people who are intensely interested in me as a friend, leader, or lover. In my mind, we have stimulating conversations, mutually plan important pursuits, and build memories together as a cohesive team.

Restless Bill also likes to look back. When I was in the seventh grade, my best friend's dad allowed us to build a fort in the attic of his garage. This was our guy hangout. We built it with our own hands, and we were proud of our place. It was a place to enjoy being young men, and there were no girls allowed, except for the intoxicating pictures of women we used to wallpaper the fort. We talked about what these women would do if they were with us in our fort. It's easy looking back to dismiss our antics as teenage foolishness. When loneliness sets in, however, Restless Bill wants to bring the wallpaper to life.

Passionate Without Regrets

We will spend the rest of our lives trying to understand our passions. We can, however, learn to live with them and prosper from them as God intended if we are willing to identify our passions, recognize how they reveal themselves through our various personas and roles, and choose daily to direct them. These simple steps, when practiced diligently, allow us to be passionate without regrets.

Step 1: Identify Your Passions

You are a unique creation of God and have been designed with a unique collection of desires that drive you forward. The individual passions are not unique, but the way they are combined in you is a one-of-a-kind expression of the image of God. To help you identify your passions, choose from this list of desires and then add your own. Remember that all of us have most of these desires to some degree. You are looking for the passionate areas of your life that demand your attention and direct your decisions.

love for God
love for family
love for power
influence
automobiles
technology
sports
business
sexual activity
intimate conversation

parenting
food
gardening
farming
hunting
fishing
ministry
friendship
training others
____
____
____
____

Step 2: Identify the Personas You Have Created

What roles do you adopt in order to express and feed these passions? Describe the healthy and the unhealthy expressions of who you are. Don't feel like you have to be too clever here. It is more important that you identify how you express your passions rather than put pressure on yourself to be creative.

The healthy expressions of who I am include:

Name I would give this persona	Need this persona is focused on	Traits of this persona	How this persona helps me

The unhealthy expressions of who I am include:

Name I would give this persona	Need this persona is focused on	Traits of this persona	How this persona helps me

Step 3: Direct Your Passions Daily

We are tempted to give in to unhealthy ways of expressing our passions because they are constantly vying for our attention. We can't just tell them to go away or make a single choice that tames the desire for the rest of our lives. The competition begins each morning, and winning will require us to seek the grace and strength we need one day at a time. Jesus himself said, "So do not worry about tomorrow; for tomorrow will care for itself. Each day has enough trouble of its own" (Matthew 6:34). The goal is to embrace the passions that make you a man and live them out with integrity, freedom, and grace.

For instance, Redeemed Bill has been called by God to love Pam with the same passion that Christ has for the church. Redeemed Bill has also been challenged to be passionate about Pam romantically and sexually in Proverbs 5:18-19.

> May your fountain be blessed,
> and may you rejoice in the wife of your youth.
> A loving doe, a graceful deer—
> may her breasts satisfy you always,
> may you ever be intoxicated with her love.

I can choose each day to embrace this kind of love for Pam or I can give in to Restless Bill who is good at replacing the real thing with a fantasy. I have seen that victory today makes tomorrow a little bit easier. All my attempts to "change this part of my life once and for all" have never lasted very long. When I make it my goal to stay focused one day at a time, I find my track record is much more effective.

Focus with Fellowship and Accountability

It is unlikely you will be able to do most or any of this on your own and in secret. I think the unspoken desire of every man is to figure out his own problems, solve them without having to expose his weakness to others, and then show off his strong position.

But this is not how God designed us. He created us to be a body, teammates who compete together, grow together, and figure life out together. Many passages in the Bible clearly explain this interconnectedness, but let me use Galatians 6:1-5 to illustrate the point.

> Brothers and sisters, if someone is caught in a sin, you who live by the Spirit should restore that person gently. But watch yourselves, or you also may be tempted. Carry each other's burdens, and in this way you will fulfill the law of Christ. If anyone thinks they are something when they are not, they deceive themselves. Each one should test their own actions. Then they can take pride in themselves alone, without comparing themselves to someone else, for each one should carry their own load.

Notice that in the passage, we are all supposed to "carry our own load" and we are to "carry each other's burdens." In other words, we are supposed to learn how to live strong by helping each other learn how to live with our strong passions.

When I was courageous enough to share the various expressions of who I am and how they help live out the passions in my heart, the tone of our men's small group changed. John said, "Redeemed Bill resonates with me because I have that same passion to help people in relationships. Restless doesn't fit me, but lonely does. I look strong on the outside, but I feel alone a lot, and it has gotten me in trouble when I don't think I can trust my wife and you guys with very personal needs." John added, "You can tell a man is being vulnerable when he admits to driving a VW convertible!"

Mike got in the discussion even though he was new to the group. "I can't imagine my life without being passionate, and I never thought about these different characters we create. It's not real clear right now, but this resonates."

Rob's Passionate Journey

Rob's response was courageously encouraging to all of us:

> As I thought about this assignment, I became aware that I have many passions in my life. In fact, life would be unbearable without them. They make me feel strong, keep me interested in life, and energize me to work hard, love my wife, and invest in the lives of my children. I have come to realize, however, that there are a number of "different Robs" that help give these passions an opportunity to express themselves. I have found it helpful to view them as categories.
>
> ***Husband Rob.*** My wife is a beautiful, smart, motivated, hardworking, and extremely loyal woman. When I met her she was a mother of two, owned a successful business, and was very complimentary of me. All these things were very attractive to me, so I popped the question. When we both said, "I do," I began to feel more complete, like there was a purpose to my life. I enjoy doing things for her, because I quickly found that service to her expresses love. Husband Rob likes sex, but he does not get to enjoy this prized activity nearly enough because we both work hard and are often mentally and physically drained by the end of a long day.
>
> ***Hurt Rob.*** This Rob reacts intensely to rejection. His father was abused as a boy and passed on the hurt with words that cut deep. When I was eleven years old, my dad told me I was a huge disappointment to my family because I didn't have the strength to hold up a bumper he was working on. I

wish he would have just hit me because that wound would have healed. That kind of experience is probably why I don't like to disappoint anyone. Hurt Rob was the fat kid in school who got beat up after school, harassed by his sisters, drank excessively during high school, and never did well in class. He never thought he was good enough and part of him still carries those insecurities.

Husband Rob and Hurt Rob switch places with blinding speed. Husband Rob seeks after closeness and enjoys being romantic with surprise gifts and flowers. It is a fragile intimacy, however, because criticism makes him feel unattractive and disrespected. When this happens, I get quiet, surly, lonely, and unloving. Affection and support are replaced with coldness and indifference. I disappoint myself because, even though I know what to do, the fear of criticism holds me back.

Work Rob. This persona can be rough. I work with men. Some have trusted in Christ but most have not. It reminds me of Proverbs 27:17, "As iron sharpens iron, so one person sharpens another." Work Rob is passionate about being a positive influence on these men. I carry a leadership position in my work, and I enjoy encouraging others to better themselves personally and professionally. Work Rob is ambitious and has high expectations. He never wants to disappoint or let others down, which can be "dangerous" when the desire to "fit in" takes over because working with men is a mixed blessing.

Internal Rob. This Rob inspires me but can also scare me. This is the Rob who loves to be active and pursue new adventures. I love scuba diving, biking, and competing. Internal Rob, however, can be explosive because he was the insecure fat kid who was made fun of for wearing thick glasses and looking like the neighborhood nerd. To prove myself, I want to be aggressive. If a guy in another car annoys me on the road, I want to pull that vehicle over and beat the tar out the driver. Or I periodically entertain an active fantasy life that imagines relationships I know are not real. As a result, Internal Rob can be hyperaggressive and make poor internal choices that are selfish and self-serving.

> Along the way, I lost respect for the need to be connected to a trusted team of men who are committed to keeping our passions focused, and Work Rob paid the price. I recently crossed a line by engaging in inappropriate verbal comments with a woman. It was very flattering to hear compliments that fed my ego, but it created a mess for both Work Rob and Husband Rob. It is a painful process to make things right, as I am constantly reminded of my stupidity. I want to move on but have a hard time forgiving myself. It has reignited my dedication to be with a team of men who embrace the passions of our lives and the potential these passions have for both good and bad.
>
> ***Dad Rob***. This is the most rewarding and frustrating part of my life. I am a stepdad by definition but not by title. To them I am Dad, even though I know my words don't hold as much weight as they would otherwise. I try to give positive encouragement and be part of their lives because I feel it is important in helping them become well-adjusted, involved, caring people. I want to be the kind of dad I didn't have—a loving, active participant. There is, however, a sharp-tongued, agitated version of me who emerges when I don't feel I have a say in how things should be done. Dad Rob has his opinions, and when his wife disagrees, it is humbling because I lose the battle every time. When she takes my advice, however, I feel like I am making the most important contribution of my life.

As men, we get it. We struggle with lust. We battle against the desire to dominate others. We love accomplishment and the love of a good woman. We love the activities in our lives that make us feel like men, and we are prone to operate in secret to get needs met if we can't find a socially acceptable way. Since we all know this, we are best served when we find a group of men who are willing to admit to the obvious and fight the battle together.

Your Band of Brothers

In the space below, write down the names of the men in your small group or in a group you would like to form.

If you aren't part of a small group, put the following steps into action:

1. Make a list of traits that indicate men are honorable enough to entrust with vulnerable details of life. Items on my list include:
    - They work hard.
    - They are involved at church.
    - They talk with respect about people.
    - They admit to mistakes.
    - They have goals.
    - They have persevered through a tough situation.
    - They can keep a secret.
    - They aren't shocked by discussions of lust, pornography, masturbation, making and giving money, or ambitious goals.
2. Ask God to introduce you to men who have adopted these traits in their lives.
3. Look for a way to get into a small group with these men.
    - There may be an organized system of groups at your church.
    - There may be community groups (Promise Keepers, Iron Sharpens Iron, Core 300) that help men get connected.
    - You could start your own group.

CHAPTER 2

Pray Like a Man

A man who partners with God unleashes the adventure in his heart.

The ability to simplify means to eliminate the unnecessary so that the necessary may speak.

Hans Hofmann

"Therefore I want the men everywhere to pray, lifting up holy hands without anger or disputing" (1 Timothy 2:8). There are few challenges on earth that get a man's emotional attention quicker than a call to prayer. When you are confident in your ability to pray, you view prayer as the most influential activity of your life. You are convinced you can move the heart of God, inspire the hearts of your loved ones, and change the course of history with the force of your interaction.

I would venture to guess that many men don't view prayer this way. The thought of praying (especially out loud in a group) is equivalent to voluntary public humiliation. When we lack confidence in our ability to speak boldly and with inspiration, we can feel something between ignorant and inadequate. We want God to be proud of us, but we think we have a better chance of gaining his approval if we keep our mouths shut.

During my years as a lead pastor, I looked for ways to help men shine. I believe men have everything they need inside to be successful in their purpose and influential in their families. I am also convinced these skills are underdeveloped or undercover because men lack the opportunity and camaraderie to bring them to maturity. I tried to help men get more comfortable with prayer by assembling a list of men to take turns closing our services in prayer. Each weekend I would call on one of them to come to the stage to pray into the microphone. This system was going well until the Sunday I called Jeff to the front.

Jeff tentatively walked up to the stage, adjusted his posture just right, and moved the microphone into a position to best pick up his voice. But no voice was heard. He stood there looking at the microphone unable to move and incapable of forming words. He tried closing his eyes as if to see if there were a recipe for courage on his eyelids, but still nothing.

The silence was becoming awkward. We wanted Jeff to succeed so we all held back for a little while. We didn't know how long to wait because this wasn't in the playbook. The hero in each of us wanted to rescue him as we frantically hoped the hero in him would emerge.

Sadly, the champion within Jeff did not arise. He stood there embarrassed, self-conscious, and unable to perform. I quickly approached the podium to close in prayer, and in that moment, I determined I would not let that happen again to men under my charge. I wasn't going to dismiss them from the privilege of praying; instead, I was going to train them to pray in a way that fit their manhood—because God wants every man to pray.

Get in the Game

As men, we have a tendency to be spectators. Many of us approach God like the crowds of men who flood into stadiums to watch others compete and complain about how the game is played or refereed. Rather than interact with God, we watch others lead worship, teach God's Word, and plan ministry while we reserve the right to evaluate their efforts.

Why do we settle for this when life is not a spectator sport? Life is designed by God to be an active, grueling, sometimes confusing, sometimes exhilarating partnership between him and us. It comes with agonizing setbacks and elevating successes. It comes with a need for persistent investigation and courageous involvement. Real joy is found when men develop the skills that enable them to hear from God and pray like men.

What does it mean to pray like men?

Men Pray in Private

Before prayer can be expressed publicly, it needs to be cultivated privately. The time a man spends in personal interaction with his God sharpens his thinking, heals his heart, and prepares him for the challenges he is sure to face on the road to his adventure. It is not complicated, however. Your personal prayer can be energized with three simple ingredients.

Prayer Step 1: Lead with Worship

When Paul challenged men to lift up holy hands, he wasn't giving a physical prescription for prayer. He is challenging us to recognize who is in charge. Teams who are successful have a head coach who is respected and obeyed. Companies that are successful respect the visionary who gives rise to the ideas and products that cause the whole organization to flourish. Similarly, any man who flourishes in prayer will generally begin by acknowledging the greatness and superiority of God.

If this is new for you, try completing the following statements as a way of training yourself:

God, you are greater than anyone in the following ways…

God, I marvel at the fact that you have no limits in the following areas…

God, I noticed that you are a great Creator this week because…

God, I praise you because your love never ends and you will never forsake those you love even though I have done…

God, I trust you because you have never been tired even after you did...

As you become comfortable with this process, you can add your own innovations that include passages of Scripture, songs, or your own unique ways of expressing your devotion to God.

Prayer Step 2: Listen Often

I find many men get bored with prayer, not because we think it is unimportant. I believe most men are convinced that prayer is one of the most noble and vital activities of life. It is just that it *feels* like a passive activity and, therefore, fails to energize a man like the activities he is naturally drawn to. Compared to competition, productivity, hunting, fishing, building, and searching the world through the Internet, prayer feels like sitting down and doing nothing.

But prayer isn't passive. The main reason it seems more like inactivity than a proactive pursuit is that we don't know how to listen to God in prayer. Any man who hears from the God of creation, author of salvation, and inventor of risk will look at prayer as an adventure rather than a boring duty. So, how do we learn to listen to the God who created us as relational beings?

Listening Skill: God, You Go First

Periodically, begin your time of prayer with the statement, "God, you go first today." Then assume any thought that comes to mind is something God wants to talk with you about. Don't worry about whether the thoughts are positive, negative, or neutral.

I fought this for a long time. I would set aside time to pray, and then I would get flooded with thoughts that were ugly, dark, and focused on areas of my life I wanted to ignore. I assumed this was Satan or his cadre of demons trying to distract me from praying as I should. Then I became a dad. I noticed that when my kids approached me, I was eager to bring up issues I knew were holding them back that they were trying to ignore. I started a habit with them that went something like this:

"Dad, can I talk with you?"

"Sure, I'd love to."

"Can I spend the night with my friend Bob on Friday night?"

"Well, I've noticed you've been lazy about cleaning your room lately and you've been mean to your brothers. Are you going to act that way at Bob's house?"

"No, Dad. I wouldn't do that."

"Is there a reason you act that way at our house but wouldn't act that way at their house?"

"I see your point, Dad. I'm sorry and I'll work hard this week at being better at home. If I do that, would it be okay if I go to Bob's?"

"If you follow through, I don't see a problem."

God is a much better Dad than I am. If I can figure out as a dad that there are issues I need to bring up with my kids, certainly God wants to bring up issues with us. It makes sense then to willingly open ourselves up to the process.

Once you pray "God, you go first," use the thoughts that come to mind to form points of conversation with God. Confess the sins that come to mind. Talk over the decisions that confront you. Admit to the fears that are holding you back. Agonize over the people you love who have real needs. Celebrate the victories. Report the areas that make you angry. Let every thought become a reason to talk with God as it gives him the opportunity to be in charge of your prayer time. Keep this going until things go silent. At that point, you can bring up whatever you would like or just close your time for the day.

Listening Skill: Fasting

Fasting is a voluntary decision to forego food (or some other basic need) for a specific period of time. The reasons for doing so are:

- Deny one of your earthly desires (eating) as an act of personal discipline.
- Use the time you would normally spend preparing and eating food to focus on prayer.
- Heighten your spiritual sensibilities to receive wisdom from God.

The choice to deny yourself a basic human need stirs up that desire and creates a need to sharpen your spiritual focus to subdue it. As a result, you are more likely to gain new insight and direction. It is, therefore, a good idea to periodically fast to heighten your ability to listen to God.

There are some simple guidelines to follow when you decide to fast:

- Confirm with your doctor that no medical issues would make it unhealthy for you to engage in a short time of fasting.
- Set a specific time. The length of time you fast is not as important as the fact that you do it. If you are new to this discipline, start with a very short period of time (one meal, half a day, or one day). As you get accustomed to this discipline, you can choose to fast for longer periods of time.
- Choose a specific plan for denying yourself food. You can skip all meals for a day. You can skip one meal for seven days in a row. You can skip sugar for forty days and so on. The goal is to deny yourself food to turn your need and focus toward prayer.
- Drink lots of water to eliminate the risk of dehydration.
- Come off your fast gently. Introduce whatever you denied yourself back into your diet slowly. If you

are going to engage in an intense fast (days without food), consult your physician first. And then I recommend that you read through all resources made available through Cru, Campus Crusade International in the United States. Visit their website pages devoted to fasting.

- Choose a positive attitude. Matthew 6:16-18 says, "When you fast, do not look somber as the hypocrites do, for they disfigure their faces to show others they are fasting. Truly I tell you, they have received their reward in full. But when you fast, put oil on your head and wash your face, so that it will not be obvious to others that you are fasting, but only to your Father, who is unseen; and your Father, who sees what is done in secret, will reward you."
- Spend the time you would normally use preparing and consuming food to pray. Matthew 7:7-8 says, "Ask and it will be given to you; seek and you will find; knock and the door will be opened to you. For everyone who asks receives; the one who seeks finds; and to the one who knocks, the door will be opened."
- Accompany your prayer with Bible reading. Jeremiah 36:5-6 sets the example. "Then Jeremiah told Baruch, 'I am restricted; I am not allowed go to the LORD's temple. So you go to the house of the LORD on a day of fasting and read to the people from the scroll the words of the LORD that you wrote as I dictated. Read them to all the people of Judah who come in from their towns.'"
- Journal your discoveries. As you fast, God will impress verses, thoughts, and plans on your heart. As you record these insights, they reveal godly direction you can have confidence in.

Listening Skill: Listen to God's Word

Hebrews 4:12 affirms, "For the word of God is alive and active. Sharper than any double-edged sword, it penetrates even to dividing soul and spirit, joints and marrow; it judges the thoughts and attitudes of the heart." Ephesians 6:17 emphasizes that the Word of God is "the sword of the Spirit." This means that the Holy Spirit utilizes the words of the Bible to guide our steps.

As you spend time reading and hearing the Bible, you will notice that some verses seem to jump off the page at you. Some of these verses help you feel better about yourself and about life. God uses these verses to encourage you because he knows life is strenuous and challenging. Other verses will bother you and create tension as they point toward some area of your life that needs to change. As you pay attention to these verses with a discerning spirit, you put God in charge of your personal growth and train yourself to follow his lead.

I find that my life works better when I practice this regularly. I hate to admit it but I need consistent reminders of how I ought to think, act, and relate to others. Let me share two examples that occurred recently. Jeremiah 32:17 was very encouraging. "Ah, Sovereign Lord, you have made the heavens and the earth by your great power and outstretched arm. Nothing is too hard for you." My year has been strenuous with a demanding schedule that has felt too hard at times. I also am facing a series of deadlines during the next three months that don't feel possible. It was good to hear that nothing is too hard for God.

Then I came across 1 Timothy 1:18-19, "Timothy, my son, I am giving you this command in keeping with the prophecies once made about you, so that by recalling them you may fight the battle well, holding on to faith and a good conscience." Initially I didn't understand why this verse bothered me because it talks about themes I love—competition and winning the battle of life.

When one of the men in my small group shared research he did on this verse, I started to understand my response. Rob explained, "Faith refers to the body of truth we believe. A good conscience is the sense of satisfaction that comes from actually living out what you believe."

Paul told Timothy he needs to "hold on" to these two aspects of life. In one of those aha moments, I realized our natural tendency is to disconnect what we say we believe from our behavior. This was big for me because I have been frustrated with the disconnect I see in so many people's lives when they say they believe in the Bible, yet they don't live very biblically. The verse bothered me because I was judgmental against these people. Rather than accept that people will naturally do this unless they put a lot of effort into "holding on to faith and a good conscience," I was sitting in judgment of their weakness. God was faithful to point out my bad attitude and restore a commitment in me to challenge people with compassion rather than criticism and disappointment. I am confident I would not have figured it out on my own. I needed God to intervene and change my perspective.

It won't happen every day or every week, but periodically the Bible will come alive in your life. You may be reading the Bible, hearing it, studying it with friends, listening to it on the radio, or you may hear a phrase that sparks a verse you have committed to memory. You don't have to go looking for it. You simply need to stay consistent in exposing yourself to God's Word. The Spirit of God is intensely interested in you and your personal growth. He will use any exposure to the Bible to guide you, remind you, challenge you, or encourage you. Keep in mind that God wants to lead you more than you want to be led. He will make it obvious so that you don't have to wonder or worry.

You can develop certain habits to get yourself ready to hear from God in his Word:

- Interact with the Bible in a variety of ways. Set a simple plan for reading, hearing, studying, memorizing, and meditating on the Word of God.
- Ask God to use his Word to direct your life.
- Keep track of the times that God's Word becomes vibrant for you. Write down the verses and your reaction each time God uses the Bible to give you clear directions.
- "Give God permission" to cause verses to "jump off the pages of Scripture" as often or as seldom as he wants. Now we know that God does not need your permission for anything in life, but this helps shape your attitude so you are more cooperative and less disappointed if he doesn't respond as often as you would like.

Prayer Step 3: Lay Out Your Desires

There are two distinct motivations for laying out your desires. The first is an aggressive determination to be honest about who you are. The second motivation and benefit to laying out your desires is to honestly and aggressively share your requests with God.

Tell It Like It Is

You are remarkably talented and ridiculously imperfect at the same time. You can dream of doing great things for God and entertain thoughts of self-destructive behaviors within seconds of each other. There are times you have been intensely focused on doing the right thing at the right time. There have also been times when you have gone off the farm and done things you would never recommend to others.

For this reason, God gave us the skill of confession. "If we confess our sins, he is faithful and just and will forgive us our sins and purify us from all unrighteousness" (1 John 1:9). When you are consistently and courageously open about your shortcomings, you gain a greater sense of your forgiveness and fire up a supernatural process of purification. As you honestly agree with God about the deficiencies in your soul, God makes you stronger, helps you think clearer, and attaches your heart to what is right.

When you try to hide your struggles from the one who knows everything, you create awkwardness that makes you look silly and creates unnecessary distance between you and God. It is the Adam effect that needs to be defeated in each of us every day. In Genesis 3, we have the story of man's disobedience to God set up by the deception of the devil. Once the damage was done, we see Adam taking the same silly approach we are tempted to take any time we wander from what we know is right.

Adam hid from God. "Then the man and his wife heard the sound of the LORD God as he was walking in the garden in the cool of the day, and they hid from the LORD God among the trees of the garden" (v. 8). God sees all and is intimately aware of everything that goes on in our lives. He knows when we wake up and when we go to sleep. He knows when we are focused and when we are distracted. He is aware of our greatest moments and our biggest failures. He is never surprised by anything we do (good or bad). And yet, we spend an enormous amount of effort hiding from him. We refuse to admit to what he already knows, and we try to avoid the grace he offers freely.

Adam instructed God. "I heard you in the garden, and I was afraid because I was naked; so I hid" (v. 10). God knows everything, and yet we feel the need to fill him in on what we are afraid he is not aware of. We explain our needs to him. We describe our circumstances in detail. We decide that some things in life are either beyond God's ability or out of his concern, so we educate him about what he already knows. I was listening to a broadcast by Band of Brothers radio when one of the hosts said, "If I am honest, I have to admit that I think some things are too hard for the Holy Spirit, so I have to take them over." We all know this isn't true, but it resonates with the delusion we all battle that God needs us to help him out.

Adam made excuses. "The woman you put here with me—she gave me some fruit from the tree, and I ate it" (v. 12). At first, it seems Adam is blaming Eve, but in reality he is saying it was God's fault for creating her. Even though it was his choice to do what God told him not to do, he worked hard to make it someone else's responsibility. I wish I could say we have improved, but we find lots of ways to avoid accountability for our shortcomings.

- "This is just the way I am. I have no choice."
- "This is too hard."
- "It's unfair."
- "I had terrible parents."
- "It didn't hurt anyone."
- "You seem to help others, but you don't help me."
- "I have tried over and over, but it never works."

Praying like a man means we admit to the obvious. We are passionate about life. At times, we focus these passions in positive pursuits that help the people we care about. At other times, these passions run amuck and threaten to destroy everything we consider important. God already knows, so there is no fear in talking with him about it!

Men Make Their Requests Known

You are a caring and creative person, so you have desires in your heart that you would like to see accomplished in your lifetime.

These desires involve the provisions that you believe will make life better for you and the people you love. Since these requests impact the people you carry in your heart, it makes sense that you would bring them to God. It would be silly to think that you would be silent about the most personal ideas you carry every day.

I recently attended the National Commission on Fatherhood, a gathering of people who have a passion to help dads be more effective in the lives of their kids. One of the men who spoke was Dr. Jeffrey Shears, associate professor of social work at the University of North Carolina at Charlotte and author of *What All Dads Should Know,* who has been researching the impact of fathers on the development of their children. One of the discoveries he shared had to do with self-regulation. When a dad enters a room and engages in rough play with his kids, he is doing more than just interrupting the family rhythm. The increased level of activity and intensity that occurs teaches young people to ramp up their focus and activity level on cue. When he leaves the room and the activity level drops dramatically, it trains young people to calm down quickly. Studies have revealed that children who interact with their father in this way show a greater ability to self-regulate their emotions and activity level throughout their lives.

When Dr. Shears shared this material, he did not do so as a professor making a purely intellectual presentation. He spoke with the passion of a father. He spoke with the urgency of someone who needed to incorporate this information into his family and felt a burning desire to help others realize how important a dad is to the healthy development of his kids. I cannot imagine someone with this kind of passion for fatherhood being silent. Of course he talks about it. Of course he demands that people listen. Of course he looks for ways to broadcast this vital truth.

Praying like a man is influential like this.

God anticipates that we will speak up about the people we care about. He also expects that we will make requests on behalf of the dreams that captivate our imaginations.

You want to achieve something on earth that is an expression of who you are. It may be building a business or building a new technology. It may be reaching out to a new nation or reaching out to local people in need. It may be assisting people in their personal growth or assisting a company in a worthwhile pursuit. Only you can identify the particular dream that stirs in your heart, but rest assured it is there. Achievement related to this dream would bring a great sense of satisfaction to your life. It makes sense that you would talk about it regularly with the one who can add the greatest value to the pursuit. It would be silly to think that you would be silent about the goals that capture your heart's attention.

At the Fatherhood Commission I also met Brian Blomberg, the chief development officer for the National Center for Fathering.[5] Brian enthusiastically described to me the Watch DOGS program they have developed in forty-six states. DOGS stands for Dads of Great Students and is comprised of fathers, grandfathers, stepfathers, uncles, and other father figures who volunteer to serve at least one day a year in a variety of school activities as assigned by the school principal or other administrator. Schools with Watch DOGS on their campuses have experienced a significant decrease in bullying as well as elevated levels of academic achievement, student motivation, and participation of fathers in PTAs and parent-teacher conferences.

As Brian reported the impact of the program, you could see the passion on his face and feel the energy rise in the room. He believes in the program and is convinced that every school ought to have Watch DOGS on guard. It would be impossible to silence him.

Praying like a man is transforming like this.

You have some dream in your heart. Like Brian, you may have experienced success in this dream or maybe you are struggling to find a way to grow it and express it. It is real and it demands your attention. Trying to ignore it would be unhealthy for you. We expect you to talk about the goals that inspire you. We expect you to recruit others to join you in the pursuits that energize you. Being silent about your dream would be unnatural, irrational, and destructive to what it means to be a man. God wants you to talk about your dream. He wants to hear the passion in your voice, he wants to see the gleam in your eyes, and he wants to feel the determination in your soul to accomplish what you know must be done while you are on earth.

Men Pray Out Loud

Powerful things happen when men pray out loud. Our words stick in the hearts of the people who love us, so it is worth the effort to work on this skill. Many of us have a hard time in family conversations. Some of the people we love talk too much. Some of them are confusing to us. Some of them seem to get upset when we try to talk to them. It's easy when we get these reactions to pull back physically and hold back our words. Prayer is more manageable, however, since most people know they are not supposed to interrupt when someone else is praying, and they are less critical of how we pray than how we talk. There is a connection, a bonding that takes place when we pray for and over those we care about.

It's My Turn, Dad

The influence of prayer is felt most significantly in a man's family. We have a tradition of saying a blessing over each member of our family as part of our Thanksgiving celebration. When our sons were young, both Pam and I would speak words of encouragement to each of them. Now that two of our sons are married, I take responsibility for the men while Pam compliments the ladies.

One at a time, I put my hand on my son's shoulder and complete these three sentences:

I have seen God at work in your life this past year in the following ways...

My hope for you in the coming year is...

I believe you will be able to accomplish this because...

I then light a candle in their honor and say a prayer over them. This was not something my parents did as I grew up, so I wasn't real sure how it would work. During my sons' teenage years, they tolerated the activity, but you could tell there was plenty of silent sighing and rolling of the eyes. When we weren't around, I'm pretty sure they even talked about it being a dumb thing to do.

In 2012, however, my oldest son, Brock, asked me, "Dad, this year can I say the blessing over my kids and pray for them? Hannah and I are good with you saying the blessing over us, but I want to do this for my family now." Victory!

Praying like a man is inspiring like that.

How and What to Pray

It is more likely you will pray out loud among your family or friends than you will pray on stage in front of a crowd. The way to build confidence in praying out loud is to focus on being effective in small gatherings. Whether you are praying for a child or for a gathering of men at church, there are simple ways to pray.

Be Sincere

Others want to hear the way you pray, not your imitation of someone else. There is, of course, a certain reverence that we all express in prayer because of who God is. But in that reverence, speak in words you would normally use. Assume God wants to hear from you. Use a tone of voice similar to the one you use with your best friends and family members. Don't try to get all the words correct, just speak from your heart.

Acknowledge the Value God Adds

If you are praying with your family, thank God for making you a family. If you are praying with a small group Bible study, thank God for his Word and for putting you all together as the body of Christ. If you are praying for a missionary or another ministry, thank God that he loves the world and has a long-term plan for reaching people with the Gospel.

Point Out the Strengths of the Person

Praying for the strengths and abilities of my children has been one of the most rewarding and powerful prayer journeys of my life. Prayer heightened my awareness of and sensitivity to the gifts God placed in my sons.

As dads, we can have a profound impact on our kids if we include their giftedness in our prayers. Next time you pray over your child, say something like, "Dear God, I thank you so much for creating (insert child's names). I can see that he/she is gifted in (describe the way in which you recognize their talent). I know that many people will benefit from this talent as (insert child's name) continues to grow and mature. Please give him/her wisdom and confidence with this gift."

At times you may be the only one who sees their behavior as a gift. My middle son, Zach, is gifted with people, but there were plenty of years when others wondered if he even liked people. I used to tell him, "You will never convince me that you aren't gifted with people. You read people as well as anyone I have ever known. If I were your age, I would want to be your friend because you are amazing with people."

With my youngest son, Caleb, I commonly prayed, "Jesus, thank you for creating Caleb. He is as talented at outlasting obstacles as anyone I have met. I know he gets bogged down with this at times because he feels like everything he starts has to be finished at a very high level. Please help him develop the ability to prioritize the demands on him so that he can put *A* effort into *A* priorities, *B* effort into *B* priorities, and *C* effort into *C* priorities. I'm excited to see what you have for him in the future with this incredible ability to outlast the obstacles of life."

After you have prayed about a person's strengths, it is good to then consider what prayer they need for life's struggles.

Pray for Recovery

Life is going to have setbacks. Your wife and kids are going to experience some significant disappointments and heartaches. Sometimes it will be circumstances they cannot control while at other times they will create their own trouble. It is easy to take an "I told you so" attitude, but it tends to alienate the ones we love rather than build bridges.

The most common heartaches people experience are goals that don't work out, relationships that break up, loved ones that lie to us or disappoint us, or health issues that change the course of our lives. At these moments our loved ones long for us to rally around them. To encourage you when you encounter these difficult times, I have provided prayers to suit different circumstances. Select and modify the one that fits the need of those you cover in prayer.

Prayer when a goal doesn't work out:

> *Jesus, thank you for giving (insert name) interest and ability in the area of (describe the goal). I am so proud of the bold step (insert name) took recently. Dear Lord, you know it didn't turn out the way (insert name) hoped it would, but I know that you never waste the opportunity to make us stronger and wiser. Please remind (insert name) that you are crazy about him/her. Please use this experience to develop wisdom in his/her heart that will bring strong guidance in the future. Please give him/her*

a glimpse of how this will work together with all the other experiences of life to bring about good (Romans 8:28). Replace any sense of discouragement with the confidence that you will never leave him/her or forsake him/her (Hebrews 13:5). Thank you for the step (insert name) has taken toward success in life because everyone who has ever succeeded has tasted defeat along the way.

Prayer when someone experiences a break up:

Jesus, thank you for relationships even though they bring pain to our lives. I am so grateful that (insert name) is interested in having a healthy, encouraging relationship with someone that loves and supports him/her. I am also so proud that (insert name) is emotionally vibrant enough to be disappointed that this relationship did not work out. Please help (insert name) recover from this heartache and fill him/her with the kind of wisdom he/she can gain only from the rugged realities of life and love. Remind (insert name) that he/she is not alone in this struggle because you are close to the brokenhearted and know intimately what it is like to have important relationships not work out.

Prayer when a loved one lied or disappointed:

Dear God, I thank you for our family and the way our relationships are a picture of your love for the church and the church's love for you. Unfortunately, we are all imperfect and do things that hurt one another. I am so sorry that (insert name) had to experience this. Please give (insert name) the ability to forgive even though he/she is really disappointed. Give (insert name) the same kind of love for people that you possess. Even though we are all imperfect and have hurt you in many ways, you loved us enough to have Jesus pay the penalty for our shortcomings on the cross. Would you please put that same kind of love in (insert name)'s heart?

Prayer over a health issue that has changed the course of life:

Dear God, you have said we should give thanks in all things, so by faith I thank you for your faithful love and your presence in the midst of this difficult time. I don't understand why (insert name) has to experience this pain in his/her body, but I know that nothing can separate us from your love (Romans 8:35-39). It is our great desire that you would heal (insert name) physically. While we are waiting, please give (insert name) emotional and spiritual strength that goes beyond his/her natural ability. We would never have asked for this, but since it is now part of our life, please utilize this experience to bring hope and strength to other people.

When you pray like a man, things happen because "the effective prayer of a righteous man can accomplish much" (James 5:16 NASB).

Praying like a man is powerful like that.

CHAPTER 3

Pursue a Plan

A man with a plan will always do better than a man who lives by accident.

Simplicity is an exact medium between too little and too much.

Joshua Reynolds

You were made to create plans. You possess the ability to think. You are creative in some way and have active problem-solving instincts. You have been given these skills because God wants you to be a full participant in your life. One of the key ways we participate fully in God's purpose is in and through our careers. What we do with our time, effort, resources, and energy matters. And there is no value or valor in leaving our careers to chance.

It's simple. God wants you to forge ahead in your purpose and in his purpose. And to do that, it takes a plan.

We Make Plans Because God Makes Plans

I have often heard, "I don't really make plans because I don't want to get in God's way. I just trust him to lead me." This sounds spiritual but it keeps us from experiencing and following a crucial, simple truth: God is a planner.

Jeremiah 29:11 is often quoted to give people hope and a sense of confidence. The verse also confirms that God is a planner. "'For I know the plans I have for you,' declares the LORD, 'plans to prosper you and not to harm you, plans to give you hope and a future.'"

Since we are created in the image of God, we are designed to also make plans. Consider the following men who are said to have made plans in the Bible.

King David

> King David rose to his feet and said: "Listen to me, my fellow Israelites, my people. I had it in my heart to build a house as a place of rest for the ark of the covenant of the Lord, for the footstool of our God, and I made plans to build it" (1 Chronicles 28:2).

Jonathan

> Jonathan said to his young armor-bearer, "Come, let's go over to the outpost of those uncircumcised men. Perhaps the Lord will act in our behalf. Nothing can hinder the Lord from saving, whether by many or by few" (1 Samuel 14:6).

Nehemiah

> "If it pleases the king and if your servant has found favor in his sight, let him send me to the city in Judah where my ancestors are buried so that I can rebuild it...
>
> "If it pleases the king, may I have letters to the governors of Trans-Euphrates, so that they will provide me safe-conduct until I arrive in Judah? And may I have a letter to Asaph, keeper of the royal park, so he will give me timber to make beams for the gates of the citadel by the temple and for the city wall and for the residence I will occupy?" (Nehemiah 2:5,7-8).

The Apostle Paul

> Paul and his companions traveled throughout the region of Phrygia and Galatia, having been kept by the Holy Spirit from preaching the word in the province of Asia. When they came to the border of Mysia, they tried to enter Bithynia, but the Spirit of Jesus would not allow them to. So they passed by Mysia and went down to Troas. During the night Paul had a vision of a man of Macedonia standing and begging him, "Come over to Macedonia and help us." After Paul had seen the vision, we got ready at once to leave for Macedonia, concluding that God had called us to preach the gospel to them (Acts 16:6-10).

Numerous proverbs also declare that it is normal for men to make plans. Here are three examples:

> The plans of the righteous are just,
> but the advice of the wicked is deceitful.
> (Proverbs 12:5)

> Commit to the LORD whatever you do,
> and he will establish your plans.
> (Proverbs 16:3)

> The plans of the diligent lead to profit
> as surely as haste leads to poverty.
> (Proverbs 21:5)

That's a lot of motivation to be a planner. We will use that motivation to answer simple questions, identify simple skills, and devise some simple but essential plans for your career and life.

Your Career Counts

Work takes up a lot of your time and energy. It can be the source of deep satisfaction as you define your purpose and follow the opportunity to be productive. When your career is a significant priority, you will find yourself saying no to people you would like to spend time with and declining activities you would like to engage in so you can work. It will test your integrity and bring all your attitudes to the surface.

You can't control every aspect of your career because you will face unexpected challenges all along the way, but that doesn't take away the benefits of planning. In fact, the benefits of planning become even greater.

In order to put together a plan for your career, you will want to ask some strategic questions. You have been created with unique abilities. God sovereignly chose to give you some talents while withholding other skills. As a result, you are attracted to certain types of work while other types of work are laborious and unduly stressful.

1. What kind of work do you like to do?
2. What kind of work do you like to avoid?
3. Where do you see God's hand of favor in your life?

Following God's Favor

Today, I am a traveling speaker and author. Most of my presentations are at marriage training events alongside my wife. In addition, we speak at parenting events, I speak at men's events, and my wife helps lead women's events. This wasn't exactly what I or we set out to do. What I planned to do was pastor a local church, which I did for years. It made sense to me to pursue a ministry career because I loved the work. Helping people learn from the Bible and grow in their spiritual lives exhilarated me. I have a strong enough desire to be a pastor that it overshadows the hassles that go along with the lifestyle.

God never spoke to me in a dream, and I didn't have a vision that led me to ministry. I never heard God speak out loud telling me this is what I was supposed to do. I just looked at the evidence of my life, concluded this was a good path for me, and made plans to be a pastor.

Along the way, I grew a lot as a man and a leader and made the effort to increase my knowledge. A big step in that direction was to ask one of my seminary professors to mentor me as a pastor and as a husband. I knew he was an author, but it didn't occur to me that he might invite me into the world of writing.

Well, he did. He approached me one day and said, "My wife and I would like to coauthor a book with you and Pam." As soon as he said it, I had the sense that I was supposed to do it, even though I had no idea what was involved in being an author.

We wrote a book titled *Pure Pleasure: Making Your Marriage a Great Affair*. Shortly after it came out, Pam and I received a phone call asking if we spoke at marriage conferences. We said yes. When we got another call to speak at another event, we began to think this extension of ministry should be in our plans. We mapped out a schedule of how many times each year we could realistically present together as we raised our family and led our church.

That was when I began to see a distinct difference in how God's hand of favor worked in my life. I would put enormous amounts of effort into the church because I cared about the work and was convinced it was my place to do so. The results from the effort I put in were positive, but they were relatively slow and laborious. Then I would speak alongside Pam at a weekend conference. While we put in considerable care and preparation, it was nowhere near the planning and labor I put into the church work. The results, however, were instantaneous and inexplicably successful. The only way to reconcile what I saw happening was to conclude that God's hand of favor was much stronger on my speaking with Pam than it was on my church leadership.

I knew at some point that a transition would take place. I didn't know when it would happen because I didn't think we could effectively raise our kids if we pursued a full-time itinerate ministry. But I could tell that God's favor was moving us in this direction.

Identifying Our Skills

After much time praying and paying attention to God's leading, Pam and I concluded that we would eventually make conference work a full-time pursuit. It was then that we set out to identify and develop the skills we would need in order to raise the chances of our success. Here is our list:

Writing. Books were going to be a big part of the process. Published works would give us the credibility to be trusted and would provide a tangible way for event planners to evaluate our message and character without having to meet with us for long periods of time. Books would also attract TV and radio interviews, which would further raise our level of exposure. Our writing would, therefore, need to be instructive, entertaining, and memorable.

Public Speaking. The unique ability Pam and I possess is to speak on stage as equals and to pass the presentation back and forth seamlessly. To maximize the impact of this ability, we needed to communicate in advance about how to volley the verbal ball back and forth, identify times it didn't work well, and then practice over and over until we could function effectively and smoothly as one unit.

Storytelling. Writing and public speaking both require the gathering and telling of stories to get a message across in vibrant, clear language. Jesus was a master at influencing others because he could illustrate complex principles through simple stories of everyday life. Since we knew this was key for us also, we took on the task of learning the traits of a strong story.

Networking. Because Pam and I do training for the most

sensitive relationships in people's lives, the coordinators who plan conferences and seminars need to trust us and the message we bring. This means we need to communicate well with them and network through trustworthy channels and honorable people. We had to determine how to engage meeting planners face to face, through social media, and by personal recommendations.

Travel. I knew we would one day spend much of our time flying to various destinations. We needed to gain a working knowledge of how to find the best deals on air travel and rental cars, navigate airports effectively, move materials from one event to the next, and physically recover quickly so we could be ready and healthy for the next venture.

None of these skills are spiritual gifts. They are life skills that can be honed and improved through persistent practice. Thankfully, the development of these skills can be built into a schedule, strategically applied, and wisely evaluated. In other words, they can be planned. We can't force meeting planners to choose us or readers to buy our books, but we can plan to do our part with excellence and trust God to open the doors of opportunity.

Your Career Plan

Planning is key no matter what stage of your career you are in. Whether you have a sense of the direction your career is heading or you have a dream of where you would like your career to go, there are some skills that need to be identified, investigated, and practiced until they become second nature. Without these skills operating at a high level, the opportunities you would like to pursue are not going to be available to you.

Identifying Your Simple Skills

Refer to the simple skills I identified as essential to the unfolding and success of our speaking ministry. Then take some time to consider what skills relate to what you are doing now and where God might be directing you next. Even if a career change is not on the horizon, there is a good chance God is asking you to focus on how to make your work more meaningful, influential, and satisfying.

Take time to explore the following questions:

- What skills do you have that you do not utilize in your current career?
- Does your current job require you to work a lot in areas that are not your strengths?
- What skills do people notice in you that you have not yet developed?
- Has God opened or shut doors lately? How do those incidents relate to your career?
- How has God challenged you to step up and use your skills and develop more skills?
- What skills need to be practiced to make your career goals possible?

Develop a Conflict Plan

Effective planning can make all the difference. You plan for things going smoothly, and then you also plan for times of conflict. That isn't being a pessimist; it's being a planner.

Consider the priest, the minister, and the rabbi who created a competition to see who was best at his job. They each decided to go into the woods, find a bear, and attempt to convert it. When they got together later, the priest began.

"When I found the bear, I read to him from the Catechism and sprinkled him with holy water. Next week is his First Communion."

"I found a bear by the stream," said the minister, "and preached God's holy Word. The bear was so mesmerized that he let me baptize him."

They both looked down at the rabbi, who was lying on a gurney in a body cast. "Looking back," he said, "maybe I shouldn't have started with the circumcision."[6]

That humorous story illustrates how a lack of planning and skill can make one's job so much harder (and riskier) than it needs to be. That rabbi probably wishes he had thought through potential scenarios of conflict!

You probably aren't headed to the woods to convert a bear, but you are headed toward the uncharted areas where possible problems and resistance could arise. Things are not always going to go well. Your wife will push buttons that trigger places of anger in your soul. Your kids will do things that make you wonder if they have any respect or common sense. Your friends will interrupt your plans. And work colleagues will make unreasonable demands. If you don't anticipate these, you are denying reality and setting up your plans to be derailed.

The Two-Plan Man

To successfully navigate inevitable conflict, you will need two plans. The first is a plan to handle the simple irritations caused by people you interact with but who aren't part of your inner circle. The second plan is for responding to the people who are an intimate, regular part of your life.

Plan One

When you become irritated or challenged by people at work or strangers you encounter throughout the day, there are simple ways to stay clearheaded and minimize the disturbance to your bigger life plan.

I have chosen to borrow a strategy from my good friend Tom Hall. He has adopted a PTP approach to these everyday irregularities, which stands for:

Positive
Thankful
Patient

The choice to stay *positive* protects our minds with a reminder that every situation involves good things and prevents our thinking from spinning out of control with negative imaginations or comments. The choice to be *thankful* protects our hearts by reminding us that we have more important things going on in our lives than the irritation that is vying for our attention. The choice to be *patient* protects our will by slowing us down before we do something we will need to recover from.

Tom recently shared two scenarios that were helped by the PTP approach. In the first, he was driving on the Southern California freeway when another motorist pulled in front of him and slowed down quickly. The driver then slowed even more so he could jet over two more lanes to exit the freeway. Tom's first thought was to greet the other driver with a well-known hand gesture, but he was stopped by PTP. He chose to think, *I was able to predict what he was going to do* (positive). *I am thankful that no one was hurt* (thankful). Then he chose to count to three before he said or did anything (patient). By three, his anger subsided and he started laughing about the times he had been in that much of a hurry to get off the freeway.

The second scenario involved colleagues at work who got heated as they described their frustrations with customers who were being unreasonable. Their misdirected blame of Tom for the customers' behavior could have ignited a heated response from Tom had it not been for PTP. He chose to think, *These guys are passionate about their jobs, which is a good thing* (positive). *I am thankful that we have customers to talk about even if some of them are difficult to deal with* (thankful). Tom then chose to wait until everyone in the room had shared their opinion before he said anything. By the time everyone had weighed in, Tom had calmed down and could think clearly enough to ignore some of what was said and strategically address the real issues (patient).

Plan Two

The second plan works well when you face challenges in the intense, interconnected relationships of your life: those with your wife, kids, extended family relationships, and priority friendships. These important, ongoing relationships call for a more structured and intricate response than the casual relationships require. You will be helped if your plan includes the following three elements: Set basic ground rules, choose a road map, and learn to set boundaries.

1. Set basic ground rules for yourself.

Most conflict arises spontaneously in an emotional surprise. As a result, our natural tendency is to be defensive and say things we don't mean and do things we never intended. Studies demonstrate that men tend to get emotionally flooded during interpersonal conflict. Interestingly, when a family is in crisis the husband (dad) feels the stress at a deeper level than his wife, but others don't think so because he internalizes it. It is very helpful, therefore, for men to develop a plan they follow when conflict presents itself. The choices he makes ahead of time about how he will proceed puts his strong emotions under his control so these intense interactions bring value to his life rather than create distance or damage. Each of us needs a way to check our behavior before we create damage where we want to create unity. My basic ground rules include:

- I will not start an argument when I am angry.
- I will not swear at others or call them names.

- I will not use the word *divorce.*
- I will not storm out of a situation in anger.
- If I am not ready to work through the issue, I will reschedule the conversation rather than neglect it.
- I will seek to finish every argument. That is, I will continue to work through things until I rediscover what I appreciate about the other person.

2. Choose a road map.

Conflict is intense because is it fueled by strong emotions. If you weren't emotional about it, you would logically problem solve together and then give each other a high five to seal the victory. Interpersonal conflict does not work that way. We get stirred up emotionally and sense fear that we will be taken advantage of or marginalized in a way that is unacceptable to us. It is important to choose ahead of time how you will approach the conflict because our emotions follow our decisions. If you begin the discussion without a plan, it is likely the emotions will take over and create a conversation that doesn't make sense to either of you. If you don't have a plan in place already, I suggest the following steps to help you SOLVE the issue:

***S**eek God together.* Pray together and ask God to give you wisdom to work through the issue. Don't worry if this is not a smooth prayer. The simple choice to include God in the process will be surprisingly helpful.

***O**pen the conversation.* Decide who is going to share first. Most arguments need time to clear the air. Nobody I know is good at stating what they are really upset about clearly and succinctly. Most people dance around the issue as they test the environment. If the environment is testy and defensive, most people will pull back and guard their territory rather than work toward a solution.

This step gives everyone an opportunity to calm down by assessing the emotional climate. If you find this difficult to do, you may choose to utilize an object (a ball, a piece of paper) to pass back and forth to designate whose turn it is to share. Whoever holds the object gets to talk while the other person patiently listens. Keep the dialogue going until you feel the environment soften between the two of you.

Look deeper. After both of you have shared sufficiently, ask, "What do you think the real issue is?" It may be the issue you've been talking about or it may be something else. It could be a reaction to something from your past or something you are afraid of. It is also possible that stress has risen in your life and you are taking the stress out on each other. Or maybe you are upset with your spouse about the best traits in his or her life. Your kids may have made a decision outside of their authority that has inconvenienced your life. You may have experienced an event that has revived emotions from a traumatic incident in your past. My experience is that once people identify the real issue, they come up with insightful solutions.

Verify options. Once you've identified the real issue, discuss possible solutions. We have found it best to write down the ideas we come up with rather than trust them to memory. If one of the ideas becomes an obvious solution and you can both agree on it, commit to it and begin to implement your agreement. If the solution is not obvious, pray together and then set another meeting to discuss the solution. This will give you a day or two to consider the ideas you came up with. Since emotions rise and fall in their intensity, time will help you think through your solutions when your emotional intensity diminishes.

Evolve problems into an answer. Get back together in a day or two to discuss a solution. Be patient at this point. Some challenges in life don't actually have solutions. You may have a special needs child who regularly creates stress in your relationship. You may have had a financial setback that will take years to recover from. You may have faced a health issue that has forced your lifestyle to change. You adjust to these stresses, but you don't actually fix them. You look for ways to grow together while you live an unconventional lifestyle, but you don't ever really return to a normal life.

3. Learn to set boundaries.

The foundation of healthy relationships is respect. Respect frees people to grow and makes it possible for the healthiest people to set the pace. Consider how respect plays a dominant role in the following verses:

> However, each one of you also must love his wife as he loves himself, and the wife must respect her husband (Ephesians 5:33).

> He must manage his own family well and see that his children obey him, and he must do so in a manner worthy of full respect (1 Timothy 3:4).

> But in your hearts revere Christ as Lord. Always be prepared to give an answer to everyone who asks you to give the reason for the hope that you have. But do this with gentleness and respect, keeping a clear conscience, so that those who speak maliciously against your good behavior in Christ may be ashamed of their slander (1 Peter 3:15-16).

The ability to grant respect to others begins with self-respect and honor. The general call of the Bible in relationships is "'love your neighbor as yourself'" (Mark 12:31). Since we are consistently called to honor and respect others, self-respect must be a foundational life principle. Note the prominence of honor in the following verses:

> Be devoted to one another in brotherly love. Honor one another above yourselves (Romans 12:10).

> Honor all people, love the brotherhood, fear God, honor the king (1 Peter 2:17 NASB).

The way to ensure that relationships have a foundation of respect is to learn to set boundaries. Boundaries are decisions you make to maintain self-respect. It is mistakenly thought that boundaries are for the purpose of protecting ourselves. Self-protection might be one of the results, but it is never the primary goal of true boundaries. On the contrary, Jesus calls us to give up our lives rather than preserve them. "If anyone wishes to come after Me, he must deny himself, and take up his cross and follow Me. For whoever wishes to save his life will lose it, but whoever loses his life for My sake and the gospel's will save it" (Mark 8:34-35 NASB).

It is always possible that you will suffer for doing what is right. It is, however, guaranteed that you will suffer for doing what is unhealthy. The question is not "Will you face struggles?" but "Do the struggles have any worthwhile purpose?"

The two counterfeit boundaries that people practice regularly are *wishes* and *walls*. Wishes are requests for other people's behavior to change, which we have no control over. As a result, they are self-defeating. The problem with wishes is that they put other people in charge of our well-being. We demand that others change so that our lives will be better. When they choose not to make the changes, we get thrown into chaos.

Walls are attempts to protect ourselves from some sensitive area of life. It may be a hurt from the past or a situation that makes us feel vulnerable. The problem with walls is they point out the areas where we can be hurt the easiest. If I say to you, "I don't want to talk about my mom," and you wanted to hurt me, where would you start? With my mom, of course, because I have made it so obvious to you.

A boundary is different from a wall or a wish because of self-control. Wishes and walls put control of who you are in the hands of other people. Boundaries establish the self-respect that enables you to have self-control regardless of the state of life. Consider the examples below to see if you can identify the differences between boundaries, wishes, and walls.

Situation: Length of a phone call

Boundary: I have ten minutes to talk and then I will have to go.

Wish: You need to cut this conversation short.

Wall: We can talk about anything except (you fill in the blank).

Situation: Child throwing a tantrum

Boundary: You have fifteen seconds to stop screaming. If you don't stop, you will be on time-out for fifteen minutes.

Wish: You have to stop screaming.

Wall: I hate it when you scream.

Situation: Ministry appointment

Boundary: I can meet with you between 1:00 and 2:30.

Wish: I can meet, but it can't go too long.

Wall: Let's meet, but we can't talk about our spouses this time.

Situation: Sensitive conversation

Boundary: If we are going to talk about my mom, I need you to listen sensitively and maintain confidentiality. Can you do that?

Wish: You need to be more sensitive!

Wall: I don't want to talk about my mom.

Set a Plan for Personal Growth

Personal growth is a mandatory pursuit. Every year we add responsibility to our lives. These added privileges of influence require more of us in maturity and skill. The choices you make deeply impact the quality of the life you live. You make your choices and your choices make you. Although it is true that circumstances are often out of your control, how you *respond* to those situations is a result of your *choices.*

You were created as an *emotional* being. Can you imagine what life would be like without your emotions? Emotions are given to motivate us to grow. In a positive sense, you are most eager and willing to go into action when you are excited, happy, or encouraged. In a negative sense, you are motivated to engage in irrational or unhealthy action when you are frustrated, afraid, or angry.

When emotions are set in motion, your energy level rises, your focus intensifies, and you become more willing to put effort in one direction or another. Personal growth, therefore, involves creating a plan to put emotional energy behind sound thinking so we maximize our influence. Emotions need to be guided because even though they are good motivators, they are not meant to lead you. Emotions can shift with every life circumstance and every decision you make. That is why making plans for your personal growth is essential. Don't let the emotions dictate where you go next. Simply stick with your plan.

Simple Steps to Stick with the Plan

To help you stick with a plan for your personal growth, you can follow four steps over and over. How is that for simple? As you read this, take note of how this might relate to an immediate circumstance in your life. You can start applying this right away.

Step 1: Identify an area of your life you want to make progress in.

Step 2: Choose to listen to some advice that relates to that area. The truth of this advice will determine its effectiveness, so be wise when choosing the advice you listen to. You may find that advice in the Bible, in books, in conversations with mentors, and in peer relationships or other resources.

Step 3: Make a decision to act based on the advice you have chosen to listen to.

Step 4: Utilize the emotional energy generated by your decision to accomplish the task at hand.

Areas of growth you may want to include in your plan include:

Your spiritual growth. What do you want to learn about God this year? What activities do you want to engage in to enhance your understanding of God and his work in your life?

Your physical health. What is your plan for staying active this year? What is your plan for eating healthy this year?

Your relationship skills. What books do you want to read this year? What classes, online courses, or seminars do you want to attend this year? What habits do you want to practice in your important relationships this year?

When Things Don't Go as Planned

You are going to make mistakes. You will say things you didn't mean to say. You will fall short in some of your best efforts. Sometimes you will even make a mess of things. In any case, you are still vital to your family, your community, and your circle of influence. No one can make the contribution to life you were designed to make, so you must have a plan for recovering from your shortcomings as quickly as possible.

Often these shortcomings are humorous and short-lived.

I Can't Believe I Said That

I was having a great time with Pam. We were laughing and getting caught up with one another as we shared stories of the week. Then, for some unknown reason, I blurted out something that was really insensitive. It was one of those moments when you realize just a little too late that what you are saying is not going to accomplish anything good. I was stunned at myself because I wasn't trying to be mean. There are times, to be sure, when my attitude is childish and I say things with a little intentional bite, but this wasn't one of them. I was enjoying Pam's company and I wasn't aware of anything that was bugging me.

Without hesitation, I followed up the insensitive announcement with, "I can't believe I just said that. That was so insensitive. I obviously wasn't thinking because I would never have planned to say what I just said."

I looked at Pam to see how she was doing, and I could tell she was a little stunned also, so I kept talking. "Really, Pam, I can't believe I just said that. I don't even believe the words that came out of my mouth. That was so weird. I didn't even have time to reel them back in, they just blurted out like they had a mind of their own. Whoa, that was really insensitive."

Fortunately, my rambling rescued the mood. What could have been a hurtful, lingering memory got us both laughing. Pam gave me the benefit of the doubt because I guess I have a long enough track record of sensitivity toward her that she accepts the principle that the tongue has a mind of its own and gets carried away sometimes.

It was a perfect example for me of the wisdom found in the third chapter of James:

> We all stumble in many ways. Anyone who is never at fault in what they say is perfect, able to keep their whole body in check (v.2).

> The tongue is a small part of the body, but it makes great boasts. Consider what a great forest is set on fire by a small spark. The tongue also is a fire, a world of evil among the parts of the body. It corrupts the whole body, sets the whole course of one's life on fire, and is itself set on fire by hell (vv. 5-6).
>
> With the tongue we praise our Lord and Father, and with it we curse human beings, who have been made in God's likeness. Out of the same mouth come praise and cursing. My brothers and sisters, this should not be (vv. 9-10).

So, what exactly did I say to Pam that was so insensitive? Well, it wasn't a good thing to say the first time, and I am not foolish enough to repeat it. You will just have to imagine what it might have been based on your own experience.

Situations like that one can be recovered in a matter of minutes if you are determined to be humble and sincere and just own up to the fact that your humanity can get in the way.

Other situations are much bigger and have a more pervasive influence on life.

Your Recovery Plan

When plans get disrupted, disturbed, or all-out derailed, a recovery plan will give you a foundation to stand on so you can regroup and press on. Your recovery needs may be simple or intense. The key is to be honest about your propensity to miss the mark and to establish a deliberate plan that helps you get back on track as quickly as you can. Everyone you know is just as imperfect as you, so they will respect you for the way you recover more than your efforts to be perfect around them. It makes you real and approachable.

Andre's story is a great example of why having a plan for recovery is not only smart but possibly lifesaving. Andre appeared to be past his addictive behavior. He was running his own business with success. His wife had confidence in him and was convinced his demons were behind him. His kids loved spending time with him and were proud to see him at their baseball games and dance recitals. Life had never been better, so he relaxed his commitment to his support network.

Then he got a big payoff for one of his jobs, and his old lifestyle screamed for attention. Without regard for a life plan or the consequences, Andre looked up his old drug dealer, purchased new product, and ended up high in a park. When he didn't get home on time, his wife put the word out to his friends, and they all went looking for Andre. They found him disoriented, panicked, and broke.

His wife was disappointed because she trusted him. She was discouraged because the family needed the money to keep up with their bills, and he had squandered it. She was angry and he was ashamed, and they were in trouble. If he didn't put a plan for recovery into place, he was going to lose everything he had worked hard to establish.

His first step was to enroll himself in a residential treatment center to detox and reset his priorities. He was hoping his wife would work with him but was determined to do this with or without her approval. Upon release from the treatment center, he committed himself to weekly meetings with others who were determined to make their addiction a thing of the past.

It was inconvenient to make this commitment, but he was determined to do this regardless of the reactions he got from family and friends. He knew his personality needed this structure, but he had gotten proud and lazy about it as he convinced himself he could handle it. He has now made it a weekly priority. He lost his business and humbly approached his stepfather to see if he could work for the family business. He had resisted this in the past because he wanted to be his own man who didn't live under his dad's authority. His new plan included the humility to admit his life would be better with his dad's help.

Today Andre is living a steady, responsible life. His marriage is intact. His kids see him every day. He is successfully working in the family business, and his support network sees him every week. He learned that his recovery plan must be consistent and structured.

No matter your circumstances, you can learn a lot from someone who faced this extreme level of recovery. Structure is needed, and a plan of action can mean the difference between living a life of deception and destruction and living the life of meaning God intends for you.

Making plans is a cooperative partnership between you and the God who created you. Your role is to make plans that engage your heart, mind, and will. God's role is to direct your steps so your plans dovetail with his plans.

Start making plans today!

CHAPTER 4

Build What Only You Can Build

A man highly values the life he builds.

Don't make the process harder than it is.

Jack Welch

Our youngest son, Caleb, is an engineer. Some of our good friends also have a son who works as an engineer. With such a unique area of shared interest, we decided it would be a good idea to introduce our sons to each other.

The meeting was a little awkward because our sons are very different. Caleb is a mechanical engineer while theirs is an electrical engineer. He is remarkable at theoretical planning while Caleb is focused on practical applications. Caleb was an athlete who competed in college football for four years. Their son is committed to participating in Comic-Con every year. It didn't take long to realize they didn't have a lot in common.

In the midst of the conversation, their son made a very interesting statement: "In my spare time I am building a 3-D printer, just for fun."

The statement changed the entire conversation. I didn't really know what a 3-D printer was, so I asked a lot of questions. He had caught our attention because he was building something. We could rally around this topic because all men have it in their hearts to build something because we are created in the image of God, who is a builder.

God the Builder

In the very first chapter of the Bible, we are introduced to God as a builder and maker of all life. The chapter ends with a satisfying statement of completion, "God saw all that he had made, and it was very good. And there was evening, and there was morning—the sixth day" (Genesis 1:31). It reminds me of the feeling I get when I finish a project.

Pam and I had one of those humorous moments of discovering the differences between us. I had just finished a closet remodel on our house. I was pleased because the doors went on correctly and they looked great. I have always had trouble getting doors to hang straight and fit without binding, so I was quite proud of the fact that these doors fit and opened and shut smoothly. I sat staring at the finished project, taking in the satisfaction of the moment. Pam came to find me and asked, "What are you doing?"

"Come look," I said.

"Hey you finished. It looks great," and then she left the room.

She came back about five minutes later and asked again, "What are you doing?"

"Come look," I said again. Of course, I was hoping to hear her say, "I have seen all that you made and it is very good." Instead, she said, "I did. It looks great. Can you help me downstairs?"

I was disappointed Pam didn't take more time to admire my handiwork, and she was confused over my need to stare at a finished project. All I can say is the finished project touched something inside me that was very satisfying.

Observations I have made in my years of interacting with men convince me that achieving this satisfaction is part of what it means to be a man. It is no surprise because throughout the Bible we see God challenging men to build and men being drawn to building. The first man God made was immediately given a building task. "The LORD God took the man and put him in the Garden of Eden to work it and take care of it" (Genesis 2:15).

The first two men born in history were known by what they built. Abel built up a herd of sheep while Cain built up fields of crops (Genesis 4:2). It didn't take long for Cain to get the idea that building a city would be a good idea: "Cain made love to his wife, and she became pregnant and gave birth to Enoch. Cain was then building a city, and he named it after his son Enoch" (Genesis 4:17).

Noah was commanded to build an ark: "So make yourself an ark of cypress wood; make rooms in it and coat it with pitch inside and out. This is how you are to build it..." (Genesis 6:14-15). The first thing he did when he got off the ark was to build an altar: "Then Noah built an altar to the LORD and, taking some of all the clean animals and clean birds, he sacrificed burnt offerings on it" (Genesis 8:20).

Nimrod was known as a great warrior, in large part because he built cities: "The first centers of [Nimrod's] kingdom were Babylon, Uruk, Akkad and Kalneh, in Shinar. From that land he went to Assyria, where he built Nineveh, Rehoboth Ir, Calah and Resen, which is between Nineveh and Calah—which is the great city" (Genesis 10:10-12).

When the people of the world wanted to unify their efforts in rebellion against God, they set out to build a tower. "Then they said, 'Come, let us build ourselves a city, with a tower that reaches to the heavens, so that we may make a name for ourselves; otherwise we will be scattered over the face of the whole earth'" (Genesis 11:4). And this is just the first eleven chapters of the Bible!

It even appears that men risk not being at their best when they are not building.

> When the LORD your God brings you into the land he swore to your fathers, to Abraham, Isaac and Jacob, to give you—a land with large, flourishing cities you did not build, houses filled with all kinds of good things you did not provide, wells you did not dig, and vineyards and olive groves you did not plant—then when

> you eat and are satisfied, be careful that you do not forget the LORD, who brought you out of Egypt, out of the land of slavery (Deuteronomy 6:10-12).

When men live in cities and houses they haven't built, there is a tendency to forget the Lord. We lose our appreciation for the process of subduing the earth and begin to believe we are entitled to an abundance of possessions.

The Process of Great Building

Some men love to build buildings, communities, cities, and the infrastructure to support them. I have friends who work in the construction industry, and I've noticed how they all take great pride in what they do. I have also noticed that men who love to build follow a pattern that inspires them to tackle the project with all its risk and obstacles. I had the opportunity to visit the London Tower Bridge recently so allow me to use this project to outline the process builders go through.

Step 1: Identify a Need

The year was 1876. The East End of London was densely populated and business was thriving. The port was handling cargo from hundreds of ships. Pedestrians and vehicles flooded the streets with the hustle and bustle of city life. People on foot could be transported by boats, but the increasing number of motorized vehicles created consistent traffic jams since the only way to cross the famed Thames River was the London Bridge. Commuters were waiting for hours to get across revealing a desperate need for a new bridge. The City of London Corporation decided they could wait no longer and made the decision to build a new bridge to the east of London Bridge.

Step 2: Decide to Take a Risk

The need for the bridge was obvious to all, but the project needed to be built without disrupting traffic and activities on the river. A special committee was formed in 1876 to determine the best way to discover a design and monitor public reaction. They presented the idea of a new bridge to public competition to harvest ideas. They were hoping somebody would come up with a truly innovative design that would service the traffic needs and make an architectural statement for the city of London. They received more than fifty designs, and after six years the contract was awarded to Horace Jones (the city architect) in collaboration with John Wolfe Barry.

Step 3: Seek Innovative Solutions

The design for the bridge is a combination of a suspension bridge with elements of a bascule bridge. *Bascule* is a French word that means "seesaw." The bridge is supported by two massive piers sunk into the river bed. The middle sections of the bridge needed to be raised to allow river traffic to pass. Water would be diverted just enough to make room to build the piers without stopping traffic on the river. Each tower is about 200 feet high. The bridge is roughly 750 feet long. Walkways were built 120 feet above the river spanning the two towers for foot traffic when the bridge was raised. Eleven thousand tons of steel and seventy thousand tons of concrete would be required to build the bridge. The cost would be enormous and the process would be challenging, but they figured out a plan that would overcome the obstacles.

Step 4: Work Hard to Drive the Project Forward

The project took eight years to complete. Five major contractors were employed throughout the time line and 432 construction workers put in time on the project. The workforce included hydrologists to divert the water, steelworkers to create the framing, masons to set the concrete, laborers to support the work, and craftsmen to install the Cornish granite and Portland stone on the steel structure to give the bridge its distinctive look.[7]

Building All Areas of Life

It is easy to think that building applies only to structures. In reality, men take on a wide variety of challenges that require building. Men build systems that help businesses and other organizations run smoothly. Men build technology that has transformed every process in our lives from the way we communicate to the way we do business to the way we do dishes. Men build equipment that makes every task in life easier and more productive. We are so accustomed to having these tools in our lives that we forget how important they have become.

Just in the last week, I had conversations with all three of my sons that included equipment. Brock spent time describing to me the new tires and gear mechanism he would like to add to his mountain bike. Zach described the combination bow he would like to get to enhance his hunting experience. Caleb asked if I had an external tachometer because he needed one for his engineering project at school. None of them talked as if having access to such things was a big deal. They are so used to having equipment in their lives it seems those tools have always been around.

As you look in your heart, you will discover a desire to build something. As you look around at your circle of friends, you will likewise discover a drive in each of their lives to build something. To illustrate, let me describe some men in my life. As we go through each of these, take note of the differences in what we like to build.

Myself

I come from a long line of tinkerers. I first saw this ability to work with my hands during high school. The pump to our backyard pool was exposed to the sun and would run hot. I decided to build a cover over it. I had never built anything with a roof. I had never helped my dad with any kind of remodel or other construction project. I just believed I could do it and set out to make it happen. That structure is still standing today, and I laugh every time I look at it. It is crude and unsophisticated, but it is sturdy.

I also took an interest in cars during that time. I also laugh when I look back because the car I dreamed about was a 1972 Chevrolet Vega. It wasn't my dream car, but we owned one so it was the only car I could afford to dream about. I admit it was a dream without wisdom.

The Vega was the first GM product developed as a generic conglomeration of parts designed by a corporate team rather than a Chevrolet product created by Chevrolet designers. Chevy's only role was to sell the car they had little ownership over. As a result, quality control was low, inspiration to find and fix problems was minimal, and the team's interest in the car was sorely lacking. The popularity of the car matched with its design flaws almost ruined the company. The engine was prone to overheating, the aluminum block was known to crack, and it was notorious for burning oil.

Nevertheless, I dreamed of turning our Vega into a performance machine. I researched modifications that would make the car faster. I read articles about putting a V-8 motor in the compact car designed to compete with foreign imports. I chose a custom paint job I would someday add.

I was deeply disappointed the day I told my dad about my plans. I explained the modifications I wanted to perform. I appealed to him to help me figure out how to pay for the upgrades. My heart sank when he said to me, "I don't think it is a good idea to modify a car. The factory made it this way for a reason, and we should not mess with it."

As a young man, I thought my dad was fearful, unimaginative, and boring. I have come to realize he just likes to build different than I do. He believes in corporations and teams of engineers. That is why he designed rocket engines for a living. His belief in the corporate environment put men on the moon!

I made minor modifications to my Vega that made it a little bit faster until I came to my senses and realized this probably wasn't the wisest choice for a performance platform. I now own the Cabriolet as a hobby because it gives me an outlet for tinkering and keeping the dream alive.

My Friends

Ken is a committed entrepreneur. He has spent the last thirty years building up his business. He has experienced seasons when the business flourished, and he has suffered through lean times where he wasn't sure where the next job was coming from. He has had so many clients at times that it was nearly impossible to keep up with the work, and at other times he has had so few clients his business was vulnerable to failure.

Ken's attitude has never changed, however. He has always believed this is the right way for him to live. He has always believed things would work out. The lean times increase his faith that God will bring the right work at the right time. The times of prosperity sharpen his focus to work harder and accomplish more.

Steve builds networks better than anyone else I know. Every time I meet with him, he tells me about a new business that has begun, a new business leader who has emerged, a new development in the life of one of our friends, or a new ministry leader who was hired. He attends three small groups and effectively keeps track of the people involved. Any time he needs to make a transition, whether it is a business move, physical move, or change to his workout routine, he meets with someone who opens up the next door of opportunity.

Jim makes music. He has a day job, but it doesn't take long being with him to realize his passion revolves around a guitar and the world of music. He collects guitars, writes music, practices incessantly, and looks for opportunities every month to play with other talented musicians.

Josh builds his life around technology. He loves his smartphone. He stores and accesses lots of information, has several intranet sites he uses for workgroups, and studies programming as a hobby. And, of course, his tablet is also his TV remote control.

I could go on because every man in my circle of friends is involved in building something or has the desire to be involved in a movement that is helping to build something worthwhile. Your circle of friends is the same way because God created men to build.

When Men Don't Build

What happens when men don't invest the effort to build? Often times, they become lethargic. It is like muscle development. If you keep using and building your muscles, they become stronger, more agile, more coordinated, and more useful. If you fail to use muscles, they atrophy into uselessness.

Years ago my friend Scott went through a messy divorce and subsequent loss of his career. He is a talented programmer and systems designer who lost focus, lost confidence, and lost his will to take risks. The first year after his divorce was spent mourning the loss of his dream and sabotaging his success. He was plagued by the thought that anything he would produce would be taken by his ex-wife, so why try. He then discovered that there were women around who were willing to support a man financially in exchange for companionship. He took advantage of that opportunity to his own detriment. His confidence to network with people in his industry all but disappeared. His ability to make excuses for himself overshadowed his desire to succeed. He became impervious to any of his friends' challenges to get back in the game, fire up his goals, and build something. He had atrophied and was unable to do what he knew he was capable of.

Then something kicked into gear. I saw it when we were talking about his kids. They were both about to enter adolescence, and we were discussing the importance of a dad in the life of a teenager. I said to him, "Young people tend to gain confidence from their relationships with their moms because they can sense that mom believes in them and is totally committed. They learn to make decisions, however, through interaction with their dads. There are a lot of young people running around today who are unskilled and insecure about making decisions because too many dads have been absent."

Scott's response was different than what I had seen from him in the past. He was intensely interested. He asked follow-up questions. He said he needed to do something about that with his kids. Then he took action.

He set up a schedule to call his kids and faithfully called every time he said he would. He started making appointments with his kids to have lunch, to talk, and to find out the significant events in their schedules. He called his old contacts to see what kind of work was available in his field, which led to more contacts and more networking.

For the past year, Scott has been busier than I have ever seen him. He is now a project manager for a consulting firm that sets up systems and software for companies. He travels quite a bit but is finding ways to spend more time with his kids than he did when he was unemployed. He works long hours but spends time every day reading for personal growth. He has a positive attitude and is effectively maintaining connections with friends. The atrophy has been replaced with agility and focus.

Think Like a Builder—Become a Builder

We established early in this chapter that God designed you to be a builder. As you seek after God's will for your life, the area in which God wants you to build will become evident. It requires training our minds. "Do not conform to the pattern of this world, but be transformed by the renewing of your mind. Then you will be able to test and approve what God's will is—his good, pleasing and perfect will" (Romans 12:2). Review the following thoughts that God says are true about you.

> In all these things we are more than conquerors through him who loved us (Romans 8:37).
>
> You also, like living stones, are being built into a spiritual house to be a holy priesthood, offering spiritual sacrifices acceptable to God through Jesus Christ...you are a chosen people, a royal priesthood, a holy nation, God's special possession, that you may declare the praises of him who called you out of darkness into his wonderful light (1 Peter 2:5,9).
>
> There are different kinds of gifts, but the same Spirit distributes them. There are different kinds of service, but the same Lord. There are different kinds of working, but in all of them and in everyone it is the same God at work. Now to each one the manifestation of the Spirit is given for the common good (1 Corinthians 12:4-7).
>
> For we are God's handiwork, created in Christ Jesus to do good works, which God prepared in advance for us to do (Ephesians 2:10).
>
> Jesus has been found worthy of greater honor than Moses, just as the builder of a house has greater honor than the house itself. For every house is built by someone, but God is the builder of everything (Hebrews 3:3-4).

God thinks of you as a builder. The more you see yourself as a builder the closer your view of yourself matches God's view of you. To help cultivate a building mind-set, ask yourself the following questions often:

1. What need am I aware of that seems to want my attention?
2. In what arenas of life am I good at building something (construction, landscaping/gardening, mechanics, networking, technology, business, etc.)?
3. What "project" do I want to work on this year?

Cultivate a Dream

One of the main reasons God put in your heart a desire to build is to solve problems in an imperfect world and to create a healthy environment for your loved ones. To keep that desire alive amidst the difficulties of life, God places a dream in our hearts that inspires us to act, motivates us to plan, and often frustrates us when we have to wait for it to develop.

Throughout the Bible, God gives men a clear calling or dream that requires them to wait for long periods of time. When Abram was seventy-five years old (the equivalent of midlife in today's world), God said to him, "Go from your country, your people and your father's household to the land I will show you. I will make you into a great nation, and I will bless you" (Genesis 12:1-2).

In Genesis 15, God repeated the dream just in case Abram didn't grasp what was going to happen: "'A son who is your own flesh and blood will be your heir.' He took him outside and said, 'Look up at the sky and count the stars—if indeed you can count them.' Then he said to him, 'So shall your offspring be'" (Genesis 15:4-5).

And then Abram waited. When he was eighty-six, Sarai and he took matters into their own hands and decided that Hagar would be the mother of Abram's son who would lead to this great nation God had talked about. The birth of Ishmael complicated their lives since it was said of Ishmael, "He will live in hostility toward all his brothers" (Genesis 16:12). However, God's plan was still intact. Abram needed to wait another thirteen years, but God finally "appeared to him and said, 'I am God Almighty; walk before me faithfully and be blameless...You will be the father of many nations. No longer will you be called Abram; your name will be Abraham, for I have made you a father of many nations...As for Sarai your wife, you are no longer to call her Sarai; her name will be Sarah. I will bless her and will surely give you a son by her'" (Genesis 17:1,3,15-16).

When Moses was eighty years old, God said to him through a burning bush, "Go, assemble the elders of Israel and say to them, 'The LORD, the God of your fathers—the God of Abraham, Isaac and Jacob—appeared to me and said: I have watched over you and have seen what has been done to you in Egypt. And I have promised to bring you up out of your misery in Egypt into...a land flowing with milk and honey'" (Exodus 3:16-17).

The need was clear. God heard the distress of his people who were in oppressive slavery in Egypt. The solution was certainly innovative. Who else but God would conceive of sending a shepherd of forty years to the most powerful ruler on earth and command him to release the people of Israel so Moses could lead them to the Promised Land?

As with Abraham, Moses was going to have to wait. It would take forty years to finish a forty-day trip, and it would be interrupted numerous times with rebellion, foolishness, obstinate reactions, and ridiculous behavior.

The apostle Paul discovered the power of cultivating the dream God puts in our hearts: "I consider that our present sufferings are not worth comparing with the glory that will be revealed in us"

(Romans 8:18). It was his version of Jesus' words found in Matthew 6:20: "But store up for yourselves treasures in heaven, where moths and vermin do not destroy, and where thieves do not break in and steal."

Our lives are bigger than the few years we spend here on earth. They are eternal and they are glorious. God has a history-wide, worldwide plan to bring salvation to all people groups, and you are part of that plan. Cooperating with God in his plan means we can't be wrapped up in our own plans, our own needs, and our own desire to control our environment. We must be receptive to his plan and his dreams, which God freely shares with his people through his promises in the Bible and through the working of the Holy Spirit in our lives.

Our job is to cultivate the dream in our hearts by putting simple skills into action.

Step 1: Collect and Review God's Promises Regularly

A powerful collection of God's promises are listed below to get you started.

> Through these he has given us his very great and precious promises, so that through them you may participate in the divine nature, having escaped the corruption in the world caused by evil desires (2 Peter 1:4).
>
> But thanks be to God! He gives us the victory through our Lord Jesus Christ. Therefore, my dear brothers and sisters, stand firm. Let nothing move you. Always give yourselves fully to the work of the Lord, because you know that your labor in the Lord is not in vain" (1 Corinthians 15:57-58).

In him we have redemption through his blood, the forgiveness of sins, in accordance with the riches of God's grace (Ephesians 1:7).

The Lord makes firm the steps
of the one who delights in him.
(Psalm 37:23)

Even though I walk
through the darkest valley,
I will fear no evil,
for you are with me;
your rod and your staff,
they comfort me.
(Psalm 23:4)

"I give them eternal life, and they shall never perish; no one will snatch them out of my hand" (John 10:28).

He who began a good work in you will carry it on to completion until the day of Christ Jesus (Philippians 1:6).

"But seek first his kingdom and his righteousness, and all these things will be given to you as well" (Matthew 6:33).

"Ask and it will be given to you; seek and you will find; knock and the door will be opened to you" (Luke 11:9).

Then Jesus came to them and said, "All authority in heaven and on earth has been given to me. Therefore go and make disciples of all nations, baptizing them in the name of the Father and of the Son and of the Holy Spirit, and teaching them to obey everything I have commanded you. And surely I am with you always, to the very end of the age" (Matthew 28:18-20).

Step 2: Write Down Your Dream

Just like Abraham, Moses, and Paul before us, everyone who chooses to trust God discovers that the dream is uncovered a little at a time. There is a waiting period to strengthen our resolve. In the waiting, the disappointments of life and deluge of responsibility can cause us to lose sight of what God placed on our hearts. Writing down your dream gives you a tangible way of reviewing it and keeping your hope alive. One of my favorite quotes is from author V. Raymond Edman: "Never doubt in the darkness what God told you in the light." Having our dream, as we understand it, written down provides a tangible place to go to when we need a reminder that God has plans for us.

Step 3: Take a Step Toward Your Dream Every Year

Some years it will be a small step. Other years it will be a large step. Either way, our will solidifies within us what we know to be true. James said, "Do not merely listen to the word, and so deceive yourselves. Do what it says" (James 1:22). Those who decide regularly to do something about their dream discover the same kind of clarity we get when we look in the mirror. Walk away from the mirror and you can think all is good, even if your hair is a mess and you have green food in your teeth. Doing something toward your dream each year also brings freedom because you get a taste of success in God's plan to bring eternal hope to people.

Simple Truths

Before we can accomplish the most significant achievements in our lives, we must be committed to living out the simple truths.

We had breakfast with our sixteen-month-old granddaughter

this past weekend. I watched as she dove into a muffin that couldn't have been more than two inches in diameter. I know she got some of it in her mouth because I saw her do it, but I'm not sure how that one muffin was able to produce such a mess. Crumbs littered two square feet of the table. The floor under her seat looked like an explosion had taken place in the kitchen. Her clothes were dusted and her face was decorated with muffin shrapnel.

It was one of the cutest things I have seen. Had she been sixteen years old, however, it would have been a different story. Her life will be guided by a very simple truth—become more mature as you get older.

When Paul was wrapping up his letter to the church in Corinth (1 Corinthians 16:13-14), he gave a rapid fire list of simple truths that form the foundation for anything significant we want to accomplish. Our goals may be more complex than these simple truths, but they are not possible without them. As I reviewed them, I thought to myself, *These are the equivalent in my spiritual life to taking a shower, getting dressed, and brushing my teeth. I want to do more than these today, but I need to do these first.*

- *Be on your guard.* I will hear things today that are not true. I may meet people whose motives are not pure. I may encounter an opportunity I have been praying about for a while. To have the proper amount of discernment and urgency, I must remain alert and watchful.
- *Stand firm in the faith.* My faith will be challenged by competing philosophies in this world, and some things in life will not turn out the way I want them to. I must wrestle with the questions on my heart and the disappointments of life from a position of standing firm in what I know is true.

- *Be courageous.* This literally means "to deal with life in a manly way." Life requires appropriate risk and strategic competition. I will face challenges today that must be met with willingness, resolve, and unwavering focus.
- *Be strong.* Life requires physical, emotional, spiritual, and relational strength. It is a journey and a pursuit that cannot be realized in front of the TV. It must be met with goals that require strength.
- *Do everything in love.* Everything works best when we look out for the best interests of others. Salvation was accomplished because Jesus loved us enough to sacrifice on our behalf. He didn't do that so we could live selfish, lazy, or mediocre lives. He set us free to be our best. We live like him when we sacrifice to help others be their best also.

It is always possible that today will turn out to be one of those spectacular days that lives forever in our minds or it may be a perfectly normal day with few memories. Either way, it will go better if I stick to the simple truths and make plans to build something.

CHAPTER 5

Act Your Age

A man's greatest opportunities are lived in the now.

A child of five could understand this. Send someone to fetch a child of five.
Groucho Marx

One unknown author does a good job demonstrating that men like a simple approach to life.

When I bought my BlackBerry I thought about the 30-year business I ran with 1,800 employees, all without a cell phone that plays music, takes videos, pictures and communicates with Facebook and Twitter. I signed up under duress for Twitter and Facebook so that my seven kids, their spouses, 13 grandkids and 2 great-grandkids could communicate with me in the modern way. I figured I could handle something as simple as Twitter with only 140 characters of space.

But that was before one of my grandkids hooked me up for Tweeter, Tweetree, Twittertwirl, Twitterfon, Tweetie and Twitterific, Tweetdeck, Twitpix and something that sends every message to my cell phone and every other program within the texting world. My phone was beeping every three minutes with the details of everything except the bowel movements of the entire next generation.

> I am not ready to live like this so I keep my cell phone in the garage in my golf bag.[8]

The simple approach men prefer for most anything creates a tendency for us to think (and hope) that life will always be the same. The way we feel early in our lives is how we believe we will feel forever. The way we approach challenges as young adults is how we assume we will always approach obstacles. The truth is that life comes in stages with unique opportunities and gifts. The more aware we are of the offerings in each of the stages—those we've been through, the one we are in now, and the ones to come—the better able we are to act our age with excitement as we reap the rewards of wisdom, experience, change, and growth.

The Idealistic Twenties

Our twenties are a time to be idealistic. Ask any twentysomething what they want to be as an adult and the dream machine kicks into gear. In the past year, I have heard the following answers:

- I want to be a head football coach.
- I want to be a missionary who reaches people who have never heard about Jesus.
- I want to lead a large corporation.
- I want to invent a new technology.
- I want to create a video that goes viral.
- I want to discover a healthy-living organization that will help one million people eat and live better.
- I want to create a new video game.

Answers I didn't hear:

- I want to invest in my kid's college fund.

- I want to save for my retirement.
- I want to keep my job.
- I want to still be able to exercise when I am sixty.
- I want to lose forty pounds.
- I want to go on vacation where there is very little stress.

God has equipped twentysomethings for the development of faith. Our hormone levels are high and we are willing to imagine great things. This is the time in life when faith takes root in our souls. It is an extremely important time since "without faith it is impossible to please God, because anyone who comes to him must believe that he exists and that he rewards those who diligently seek him" (Hebrews 11:6). This is the time of life to ask big questions about purpose and possibilities. Important decisions will be made during this phase that will create twenty- to thirty-year commitments. It is unfair but it must be done.

Idealistic Action Points

Ask yourself,

- "If I could do anything and would be guaranteed success, what would I want to do?"
- "What would I be willing to die for?"
- "What am I willing to live for even if it leads me to exhaustion or significant personal sacrifice?"

A Note to Pragmatists

Yes, the idealistic thinking of twentysomethings falls short of reality. Yes, they are dreamers. Yes, they often pursue adventures that will never work out. It is not useless, however. Dreaming of what could be with God's help is a necessary step to building faith.

Of course, it needs to be tempered with wisdom and guided with knowledge, but it has to be there first. With good intentions, we tend to squelch the development of faith in those in their twenties. We say such things as, "You are just dreaming. You need to face reality. We've tried this before, and although we appreciate your enthusiasm, we know you're wasting your time." So, feel free to share the need to add caution to the pursuit, but don't make the mistake of thinking caution can replace the confidence that faith produces.

The Industrious Thirties

Life relentlessly marches forward. Most of us get married, develop careers, and have children. This leads to commitments that might be more difficult than we anticipated. Becoming a parent ushers in sleepless nights, endless interruptions, laughter over ridiculous things that are said and done. Selflessness stops being a topic of discussion as it becomes a necessary way of life. This is a season of productivity and pursuit.

As a result, our thirties are a time to be industrious. Our careers need lots of effort. Our families need our presence and provision. Our kids get involved in schools, youth sports, community performances, and church ministries. Each of these pursuits needs leaders, and we are likely to be recruited. We are physically strong so we are able to say yes to most of these opportunities.

During this phase of my life, I thought I was invincible. I was the lead pastor of a local church, built a home from scratch, was the president of our youth basketball league, began writing books, and spoke at marriage conferences with my wife. Amazingly, it all seemed possible. I would sleep most nights because I knew I was supposed to, but every once in a while, I would stay up all night to finish a project or get caught up on nagging responsibilities.

I see now that this wasn't the best way to take care of myself, but wisdom tends to come later. It seemed to be necessary at the time, and honestly I am not sure how I would have done it differently. Life required a lot from me, and my actions and decisions affected the people I carried on my heart. If I didn't perform well, I was sure that my family would suffer, my wife would be disappointed, my kids would miss out on opportunities I thought they needed, and I would feel like a failure.

For most men, this time of shifting into manhood is also their introduction to a life that revolves around the needs of others. We work hard, but the goals are different. No longer is our focus only on the cars we drive, clothes we wear, and places we want to go. In my thirties, life became about a yard for my boys, a place my wife could affectionately call home, money for my kids' education, and life lessons to turn my boys into men. I had a new set of goals and unlimited energy to pursue them. I was amazed at how hard I was able to work and how willing I was to do the work.

This is the point of the thirties. It is the time to build a foundation for our families. It is the time when we solidify our careers so they have lifelong earning power. It is the time we invest in our kids' growth and development so they become responsible young adults. It is the time we build our lives to gain the respect of our family members and significant peers.

Industrious Action Points

- Thank God every day for the people that matter to you.
- Thank God every day for the work you are able to perform.
- Go on a date with your wife (even if you don't go out, spend some time each week focused on your relationship rather than on your work).
- Schedule regular time with your family (the business of life will steal this if you don't!).

The Intense Forties

Somewhere in our forties things begin to change. The unlimited energy of our thirties diminishes as our bodies begin to change. Testosterone levels drop with both positive and negative results. There is a calmness that alleviates the crazy demands of our sex drive and preserves the aggressiveness in our souls for worthwhile pursuits. For many men, this brings panic to our souls because we feel weak. Since puberty, strength has flowed to every inch of our bodies from the soles of our feet to the edge of our fingernails. So, by default, we try to depend on our strength to overcome obstacles, take care of the people in our lives, and move forward in our commitments. But when that power feels like it is no longer accessible, we either learn to rely on wisdom or we frantically look for a way to get it back.

A friend of mine said recently, "My body won't respond like it used to and it makes me angry." That sums up the agony of the physical changes that contribute to the complication of midlife. Of the three forces that put pressure on people to become self-absorbed and discontent during their midlife years—career reevaluations, physical changes, and developmental mandates—I believe that transformations in our body are the most difficult.

What Our Wives Go Through

Women have an "advantage" since they deal with physical changes throughout their lives. The monthly menstrual cycle makes change a normal part of their experience. Pregnancy brings great changes to a woman's body (as well as to the marriage and family). Then perimenopause announces the onslaught of the coming midlife years, which is also the most influential time of life. Finally, menopause is a dramatic time of change where symptoms can range from hot flashes to osteoporosis and cause discomfort, challenges, and a sense of interruption to a woman's life.

I've watched Pam wrestle with many of the symptoms for the past couple of years, and I can tell it is unnerving. Out of the blue, she blurts out, "It is so hot in here. Are you hot? Is it just me or is it burning up?" It has been frustrating to her but it hasn't surprised her. She knew it was coming and she researched it for months before it began. Her midlife friends had talked with her about "the change" that was coming for all of them. Her mom had talked about the way menopause had affected her life. Pam even wrote about it in books and spoke about it in conferences. Although it has not been pleasant, it was not unexpected.

When Men Face Change

Men have unique emotional struggles at midlife based on their lack of experience with physical change. Puberty is a big time of change, but from ages eighteen to forty, things are relatively static since testosterone levels remain fairly steady. The obvious influence of this strength hormone includes bigger muscles, facial hair, a deeper voice, and a generally more aggressive approach to life. Testosterone makes men feel incredibly strong to the point of invincible as we become aware of a forcefulness that resides within us. It seems we can take physical risks without fear because we will either avoid injury with remarkable agility or recover so quickly that any damage will be minor. In every competitive pursuit, physical challenge, problem to be solved, or business deal to be leveraged, men rely on strength.

Then it happens. We wake up one day without the same intensity—mysteriously it diminishes. Although we may have heard that our testosterone levels would change, we weren't really listening and didn't believe it would actually happen, and so we were ill-prepared. I remember when it started in my network of friends, especially in Fred's case.

Fred had a heart attack the only way a forty-year-old can. He was driving home from work when a sharp pain started in his chest and radiated down his left arm. He told himself, *I think I'm having a heart attack. This is probably the last time I'll be able to eat a meatball sandwich and the sub shop has a special—two for the price of one!* Fred stopped to buy two sandwiches. He polished one off on the way home to pick up his wife and the other on the way to the hospital. Sure enough, he had a heart attack and those were the last two meatball sandwiches he enjoyed.

When the news of Fred's fate made its way to all of us, our illusion of invincibility was shattered. We all wondered, *Could that have been me?* It wasn't long before I started to notice changes in my body. I was gaining weight even though I was eating and exercising the same as I had been. My reflexes slowed down, my stomach was getting rounder, my hair was subtly getting thinner, and my joints began to ache.

One of the most disconcerting changes was the loss of endurance. Up until age forty-five, I went to bed at night because I knew it was important. Now, I found my body started demanding that I stop working every night. I was out of steam! I knew this was normal, but it didn't feel right! I became angry with myself and wanted things to return to normal, so I started running more. When the results failed to surface, I started thinking, *I wonder if something is wrong with me? I have always been able to keep my weight under control. I need to go see my doctor.* When the doc told me "This is normal for a man your age," I was crushed. I never thought anyone would refer to me as a "man your age."

I then had to admit that my sex drive was going through its own transformation. The midlife sex drive is not what we are used to (evidenced by the deluge of erectile dysfunction commercials). I was still passionate about my wife, but the sense of urgency was gone. It was okay if we waited; frequency was no longer top priority. The pressing drive to have sex was replaced with a more contented desire to have satisfying encounters with Pam.

I found sexual calmness to be a refreshing midlife gift. A man who views this as an opportunity to learn new skills and enter a new season of love with his wife will discover a new depth in his marriage. He'll find relational treasures and physical comfort with the one he's traveled the entire intimate journey with.

However, a man who cannot accept this time of change may panic over the diminishing sexual longing. He is afraid of feeling weak, unmasculine, or unable to perform, and may go looking for a new adventure to reignite his passion. He convinces himself it must be the familiarity of his long-term relationship rather than an actual change in his body's chemistry. If he acts on it, he finds a short renewal of passion—but it isn't long before it catches up with him. He cannot keep the same pace he did when he was young. The new round of sexual exploits includes failed attempts at intimacy, which reminds him of his age. Eventually, he realizes it would be easier if he returned home. Sadly, it's not always possible because of the damage he's created during his fruitless pursuit of youth.

To keep from feeling frustrated about physical changes, you can work to:

- Be content with doing less.
- Practice marital relationship skills that include interaction, patience, and being with your spouse without the need to engage sexually.
- Place more value on influencing other people's lives and less value on what you can accomplish with your own strength.

It takes focus, but it gets more comfortable every year. I spent the twenty-five most productive years of my life relying on the strength God put in me. I now have to allow the skills of wisdom and insight to mature, rely on them, and share them freely with others over the next twenty-five years.

My daily prayer is, *Lord, help me make the transition from physical strength to wise influence with grace, dignity, and integrity.*

The New Midlife

In our world, midlife has become a major issue for most people because the life expectancy curve has changed so dramatically. Currently, the average American expects to live until age seventy-nine or beyond.[9] To put this in perspective, the average male expected to live about forty-eight years in 1900 and about sixty-seven years in 1960.[10] Today, we are at the peak of our lives when people in the past were winding down. With this modern reality, we approach our fifties with more reflection, concern, and questions than our predecessors probably did. For most of us, this time of retrospection will kick into gear during our forties, while for some it may begin even earlier. When the tension between what life was and what life will and can still be kicks in, you will notice that:

- You evaluate your life more often than you used to.
- You become aware that your body does not respond or recover like it used to.
- You long for others to be more sensitive toward you and to pay more attention to your needs.
- You consider doing things you would never have considered ten years earlier. These can range from taking more personal days at work to higher risk hobbies to intense pursuit of goals that have been on hold to new relationships that make you feel better about yourself.
- You are looking for something even though you are having trouble defining it.

Since midlife is really a battle for the most prominent years of our lives, it must be faced strategically as a developmental transition, a spiritual struggle, and a social milestone. People who have a planned strategy tend to see midlife as a great time of opportunity, while those without a clear strategy tend to be surprised by the onslaught of these powerful needs.

Prior to midlife, a man is consumed with desires and ambitions. He pursues these with vigor because he feels strong and loves aggressive approaches to whatever comes his way. He is able to ignore the negative impact of his choices because he has plenty of energy and he recovers quickly. He also tends to be consumed with his interests and responsibilities to the point that he ignores his personal growth. He is gaining proficiency in his career and his hobbies but is probably lagging behind in developing relational skills, spiritual sensitivity, and balanced emotional vibrancy. Prior to midlife, these issues are boring, irritating, or unattractive. When they become driving passions later on, he is ill-equipped to their demands.

We are told that Satan is the prince of the power of the air, which means he is the designer and orchestrator of the atmosphere of this world we call home. He is actively working to keep men distracted in order to increase their vulnerability just prior to their best years. Jesus had his encounters with the devil during his forty days in the desert. And many men will have their encounters with Satan during their forties. You will discover that as midlife comes crashing in, the devil pours on the guilt and shame.

"You are such a loser."

"You didn't plan very well for this."

"You always thought you were smart, but look at all the dumb choices you've made."

"Your wife doesn't really like you, and your kids think you are a loser."

"There is so much more that you should've accomplished in your life."

And then Satan shatters with selfishness:

"You deserve better."

"You worked so hard and no one really appreciates you."

"They just want to take and take and take."

"If you stay in this situation, you'll never be happy or discover who you are."

"You need to escape before it's too late."

John 8:44 describes Satan as the father of lies. It is his nature to deceive, so it is no surprise that many men in midlife believe thoughts that others recognize as false. But to a man who is ill-equipped spiritually, these are devastating pronouncements of a shattered life. The accusations dog him relentlessly and flood his soul with feelings of failure, disappointment, suspicion, and self-absorption. He begins to believe that he is the most important person in his life and that he has neglected his own needs and allowed himself to be taken advantage of by the people he used to cherish. These thoughts are so real and personal that he fails to recognize them as a spiritual assault on his life. He feels as if he has come to his senses when in reality he is flooded with lies that are designed to wreak havoc.

Sadly, while this is happening, a man will view all of his life through a lens clouded by lies. His family relies more than ever on his growing productivity. They like what his career provides and they have no desire to see it shrink or change. Their wants are growing, so their demands on the most significant man in their lives are growing too. They don't notice the crushing weight of their needs on their husband and father because they see their requests as legitimate and fair.

His once flirting and complimentary wife now complains more than he ever thought she would. This once faithful confidant no longer listens patiently; instead, she reacts quickly to any sign of weakness and challenges him to action without trying to understand what he is going through. She, of course, is unaware of her impact on him because she is simply looking out for the needs of the family. His competitive work environment has prevented him from forming any true friendships there, and his lack of personal growth has limited his personal friendships. He feels he has no one trustworthy to talk to, which makes him vulnerable when he receives attention from another woman who seems to have plenty of time and interest in him.

Is it clear yet that the forties can be intense?

If you are in this part of your life journey, you have likely proven yourself to be proficient in various areas of life, and many people depend on you for guidance and support. Much of this season of life is hard work and lacks the sense of fun that you used to experience. And, ready or not, you are moving toward your most influential time, which will require a more mature approach to life. Adopting an intense, can-do attitude in this phase will keep you on track.

Intense Action Points

- Make it your ambition to survive the midlife transition with your career and family intact.
- Expect the battle to be intense at some point in your forties.
- Look for a small group of men you can trust. These should be guys who can keep confidences, share your goal of keeping life intact, are willing to be appropriately open about their struggles, pray sincerely, and are looking to be connected with other men. Once you find these men, commit to meet weekly (or as close to this as possible) to learn together and encourage one another on your journey.
- Educate yourself with the resources at Midlife Dimensions (www.midlife.com).

- Determine in your heart that you want to be influential in your fifties and sixties.

The Influential Fifties and Sixties

The most influential decade of people's lives today is their fifties, and the second most significant decade is their sixties. This may be surprising to you, but it does make sense. Our potential is greatest at these ages because we have enough life experience to recognize our areas of strength as well as areas of mediocrity. We have earning power that enables us to fund our pursuits. We have less personal responsibility as our children grow up and pursue their own lives and careers.

Maturity allows us to focus on what we do best while we leave other areas to people with different skills. It is at this stage that we influence others at a life-changing level. It is also why the transition from our forties to the fifties has so much turmoil. There is a spiritual, personal, and societal battle trying to keep us from our place of influence.

Once you resolve the battle of your forties, you rise up in your fifties ready to embark on your journey to influence. This is the phase of life I find myself in. One of my greatest desires in life has been to help people grow in their important relationships. During my thirties and forties, I worked as a pastor in a local church and experienced this to some degree. As I look back, however, I realize I overworked the process.

For years I experimented with ways of describing my mission, but it was too long, too hard to remember, and even harder to implement. My first serious mission statement was four pages long with lots of details and descriptions. I had the energy to push it, so I kept trying to explain it to people so they would get excited about it and help me change the world. Most people couldn't stay with it, however. They respected my enthusiasm, but they weren't confident in how they fit in.

The frustration of others not getting it haunted me for years. Interestingly, the comment that got my attention and motivated me to change things was from a plumber friend of mine. We were developing a plan to build a new church building. He and I were having a casual conversation when he said, "Well, Pastor, I am glad you are finally getting a building of your own."

I know he meant well and was trying to encourage me, but it bothered me that he thought this project was about me. I thought it was about us. I thought the whole church was pulling together because they believed in what we were doing. His comment made me realize that my level of influence was much smaller than I realized. I started asking what was wrong. I spent many days asking why my desire to inspire others hadn't reached the level I dreamed of. In the process, I came to the conclusion that my plan was too complicated.

So I started praying for wisdom and looking for new ways to expand my influence.

A Simplified Mission

Today if you asked me about my purpose, I would tell you that my mission in life is to help as many people as possible grow in their most important relationships (which include God, spouse, kids, and circle of influence). That's it. No long descriptions. No pages and pages of explanation. Just a simple commitment to help people be better at the relationships they care about.

I wish I would have figured it out in my thirties, but wisdom can't be quickly acquired as if it is an online product. It must be cultivated over time, corrected through life experiences, and conditioned with a good dose of humility. It took all the hard work of my thirties and the intensity of my forties to bring me to a place where I was willing to do what I do best and trust God to lead others to do the rest. Since that time, I have noticed a marked increase in my level of influence. I do fewer things today than I did ten years ago, but they have a bigger reach.

The most satisfying growth in my influence has been at a more personal level. My sons are old enough that we have been able to build genuine friendships. The adult friendships really launched when I began to notice that they are better at some things than I am. As I complimented them in the areas of their strengths, it softened our relationship. It seemed to validate that they had developed an identity apart from their dad so it freed them and me to engage with mutual respect.

In the past couple of years, each of my sons has asked my advice in marriage, parenting, friendship, leadership, and finances. During that time, they have added valuable insight and information to my life in areas of nutrition, workout routines, leadership, strategic planning, and vehicle maintenance.

Then there are the grandkids. I have three and the confidence they have in me is astounding. They treasure our time together, honestly believe I know what I am talking about, and naturally copy my behavior. I can tell that one of my roles in their lives is to encourage the dream in their hearts. Each of them has a love for life that is vibrant, captivating, and a bit taxing on their parents. Dad and mom have to work to build disciplined habits, keep the house functioning, oversee a busy family schedule, and discipline obstinate attitudes and actions to teach their children life skills.

That is why God created grandparents. My kids are turning out to be good parents, so I don't have to worry about the day-to-day development of my grandkids. I am free to laugh at their stories, play silly games, shoot the basketball and kick the football for two hours, play dress up, admire their creativity, and applaud their awkward talents. It is easy to be crazy about them, and I can tell it makes a difference.

My daughter-in-law Hannah recently told me, "Thanks for playing with the kids for so long. I just run out of patience for it."

I get it because I remember the busyness and focus of raising up a young family. Parents simply do not have the time or the energy to keep up with work, the family budget, kids' homework, church involvement, extracurricular activities, yard work, personal health, and dream about the potential in their children.

My time with the grandkids would be different if I had to do all the parenting too. I have great empathy for those grandparents who, for one reason or another, have had to take on that role. It is awesome for the kids because they are getting the instruction, provision, and discipline that is so vital to their development. If we have to choose, it is more important that kids get parenting than grandparenting, but it is amazing when they can get both. Those who have taken on this parenting role need to be commended and supported. You may not see the benefits in your life, but the investment you are making today has the potential to change three generations. As you invest in their lives and pray for God to lead with strength and wisdom, it is likely your grandkids will highly value family and will begin a trend where their kids and grandkids benefit from interaction with both parents and grandparents.

Influential Action Points

- Identify your strengths based on your life experience.
- Deliberately make commitments that take advantage of your strengths.
- Deliberately let go of any responsibilities you can that don't line up with your strengths. Caution is in order here because none of us gets the privilege of doing only what we love to do. The goal here is to fill our lives with our strengths and minimize the time we need to spend on weaknesses.

- Pray for God to raise up others who will do what you are not best at.
- Look for people who want to learn from you.
- Make appointments with these people (either for events or one-on-one meetings) and give them the opportunity to ask you questions that interest them.

The Indelible Seventies and Eighties

My dad is turning eighty-five this year, and his greatest moments are when he is telling the story of our family. I asked him if he had any insight into why all the men in our family love to tinker and work on projects.

"I don't think I ever told you, but my dad loved to work in his wood shop. He built furniture and wooden toys. He was very fair-skinned so he wasn't comfortable outside very much, but he loved to tinker in the shop."

"How about travel? I find it interesting that Lorraine, Jim, and I have all traveled extensively. Is that common in our family?"

"You know your mom and I traveled to Europe early in our marriage. I was stationed in France during the Korean War. I flew over before your mom. We were in Chaumont for training. Mom and a couple of the other wives flew to London. We were supposed to meet up with them and then all go to France together. Well, we were tied up in training, so the ladies got to London before us."

Mom enthusiastically jumped in, "We were looking through shops when three young European men approached us and tried to pick us up."

Dad exclaimed, "Hey, you never told me about that! It doesn't surprise me, however, because you were quite a catch."

Mom laughed and added, "We weren't interested, of course, but it was fun to be noticed."

"We had a great time. I flew missions for two years. Lorraine was born at the army hospital in Germany and we got to see much of the countryside during our free time. I loved flying most of the time. The one thing I didn't like was solo night flights to sharpen our instrument capability. When your plane gets over the Atlantic Ocean in the middle of the night, there's nothing but dark. No visual help and no landmarks. Just you, your plane, and your instruments. All you could do was trust and hope it turned out well."

I could go on forever. Suffice it to say that I'm learning some fascinating truths about my family heritage. I am equally amazed at how much I love to hear my dad talk about it. I hang on every word and am disappointed every time we have to stop. It wasn't true when we were a young family. My dad didn't have the time to sit around telling these tales, and I wasn't respectful or interested enough to listen. It is amazing how much confidence I gain from this knowledge of my family background. I wondered for years why I was interested in certain areas of life while I found little attachment to other areas. I now can see that much of it is tied to family influence.

Our seventies and eighties are a time to impart indelible memories and wisdom. The goal is to tell stories about your life, your family history, and God's faithfulness in a poignant and memorable way. People who are close to you trust your perspective and remember much of what you say.

At this point in your life, you are probably experiencing a loss of energy as simple activities now take more effort than ever before. At the same time, you are more believable than ever. You no longer need to produce at a high level. You no longer need to leverage situations to provide for your family or promote your career. Your loved ones sense a renewed sincerity, and they assign higher credibility to your words. As a result, they remember your stories with fond affection and gain strength from the best of your family legacy.

Indelible Action Points

- Tell stories from when you were the age of your kids.
- Tell stories about trends in your family. Include positive traits such as work ethic, accomplishments, spiritual integrity, and interests. Also include negative habits that are prevalent from one generation to the next, such as alcohol or drug use, divorce, anger, and the like. This way your family will know natural strengths and points of vulnerability.
- Describe the significant people in your family history.
- Recount God's faithfulness at specific points of your family history. Include times of physical protection, spiritual instruction, financial provision, and ministry influence.

How to Become a Great Storyteller

Choose a point to the story first. Is this a story of God's faithfulness, a habit to be avoided, a description of a significant influence on your family, etc.?

Choose details that support the point of the story. It may be fun to add details that don't relate to the point, but it has more impact when most of the story supports the main point.

Look for a punch line, an emotional statement that captures the impact of the story. It may be funny, sad, profound or quotable. For instance, I could tell you that young people are looking for role models to help them in their spiritual growth or I could tell you that when my oldest son was four years old, he said to me, "As soon as Jesus gets out of the Bible, I will ask him into my heart." His statement convinced me that my main role is to live out the truth of God's Word so that the people I love can see what it looks like when Jesus is alive in a man's journey.

Each season of life is a gift, so becoming skilled at acting our age is important. That way we avoid being like the turtle who, while crossing the road, was mugged by two snails. When the police showed up, they asked him what happened. The shaken turtled replied, "I don't know. It all happened so fast."

CHAPTER 6

Be a Skilled Lover

A man who is love-wise changes lives.

Enjoy the little things, for one day you may look back and realize they were the big things.

Robert Brault

Pam and I were preparing to speak to a group of parents on talking to their kids about sex. We asked ourselves, "What was our goal for our kids in this area?" It kind of surprised both of us when we concluded that one of our goals was that our sons would grow up to be skilled lovers. We wanted their future wives to be glad they married them for meaningful times in life, in personal interactions, and in the bedroom. It felt uncomfortable to actually say it out loud, but the thought strongly resonated with both of us.

Most parents face this conversation with fear. They want their kids to avoid bad decisions, moral mistakes, and the complications sexual activity outside marriage brings to the entire family. This negative approach tends to breed a mysterious curiosity surrounded by fear, neither of which is good for establishing a healthy love life. High goals, like wanting our kids to be skilled lovers, provide motivation for growth and a reason to set healthy boundaries that protect the gift. It also creates an environment where it is okay to talk about sex in a natural and enthusiastic way. If we anticipate that sex is going to be a good part of our kids' lives, we can be positive, lighthearted, and appropriately transparent about it through every stage of development.

Then it occurred to me, if this was our goal for young men, it must be a goal for my life also. As Howard Hendricks is famous for saying, "You cannot pass on what you do not possess." If I was going to help my sons become skilled lovers, I was going to have to model what that means.

From the title, it may sound like this is going to be a chapter about sex, but love is a much bigger topic than that. For most of us, the skills of building relationships and loving and encouraging others have become a lost art. We mistakenly think that being a lover applies only to bedroom activities. It certainly includes that if you are married, but a skilled lover has learned to invest himself in his most intimate relationships as well as in the people on the perimeter of his life. A good lover is a man who recognizes his needs are not the only needs. He is a keen observer who investigates how others work, think, believe, and receive value from their interactions.

This was the brilliance of Jesus who loved people like no one before him. As you adopt his example of investing in people, your wife will be grateful, your kids will respect you, your friends will admire you, and people you meet will be drawn to you. Those are the rich rewards of a skilled lover.

Investors or Consumers?

We live in a world that teaches us to be consumers in relationships. We are encouraged to seek out people to make us happy, provide satisfying sexual experiences, enhance our confidence, meet our needs, and serve our goals. There is nothing wrong with these needs getting met in God-honoring ways, but relationships go stale when they are treated as commodities. The consumer mentality is clear in the reasons people give for giving up on relationships:

"I wasn't happy any longer."

"If she really loved me, she would be more cooperative, especially with our finances."

"My kids don't appreciate anything I do. I'm sure they aren't going to miss me."

"My church doesn't meet my needs anymore. They are more focused on people who are younger than me."

"People at work don't seem to even notice me. I'm smarter than most of them, but they never want my opinion. Instead, they're content to fumble along on their own."

"My wife doesn't appreciate what she has. She keeps making demands on me, but she doesn't realize she's going to lose me if she doesn't start paying attention to how she can meet my needs."

In contrast, Jesus challenges us to be skilled lovers who are strong in our sacrifice and attractive in our selflessness.

> "Greater love has no one than this: to lay down one's life for one's friends" (John 15:13).
>
> "By this everyone will know that you are my disciples, if you love one another" (John 13:35).
>
> Let no debt remain outstanding, except the continuing debt to love one another, for whoever loves others has fulfilled the law (Romans 13:8).
>
> You, my brothers and sisters, were called to be free. But do not use your freedom to indulge the flesh; rather, serve one another humbly in love (Galatians 5:13).
>
> Now that you have purified yourselves by obeying the truth so that you have sincere love for each other, love one another deeply, from the heart (1 Peter 1:22).
>
> No one has ever seen God; but if we love one another, God lives in us and his love is made complete in us (1 John 4:12).

When you realize how much love is emphasized in the Bible,

you realize that one of the manliest things you can do is to become a devoted lover.

> Dear friends, let us love one another, for love comes from God. Everyone who loves has been born of God and knows God. Whoever does not love does not know God, because God is love (1 John 4:7-8).

Since God is love, it is impossible to know him and walk closely with him and not develop a growing ability to love the people he has placed in your life. The more God gets ahold of your life, the more you will be motivated to sacrifice for others as a demonstration of love.

Skilled Lovers Pursue Moral Excellence

Titus 2:11-12 says, "For the grace of God has appeared that offers salvation to all people. It teaches us to say 'No' to ungodliness and worldly passions, and to live self-controlled, upright and godly lives in this present age." Jesus came so he could apply his grace to our lives resulting in eternal salvation. This grace has two distinct sides to it that transform our lives and set us free to live with excellence.

The first side is forgiveness, which most of us are familiar with. We have heard many times that Jesus died on the cross to pay the penalty for our sins so we could be forgiven. This is a transaction that takes place in the court of heaven. There are three words used in Romans 3 to describe this transaction.

The first is *justified* (v. 24), which refers to a legal transaction. The picture here is that all of our sins were taken out of our file and put in the file of Jesus, as if he were guilty of those sins. Jesus then paid the price for all sins for all time so there is now a record of complete payment in his file. He then makes a copy of that payment and places it in our file. When God, as our judge, looks at our file, he sees that everything has been paid and we are reckoned to be as righteous as Jesus.

The second word is *redemption* (v. 24), which came out of the first-century slave market. If you had the resources, you could pay a sum of money to redeem a slave from the market thus setting him free.

The third word is *atonement* (v. 25), which is represented in the sacrifices that were a part of the Old Testament law. When the blood of a lamb was sprinkled on the altar, it removed God's righteous anger from the people since their sins were atoned for. Atonement is reconciliation with God.

The good news is that we are now forgiven all our sins, free from having to say yes to sin, and we have a friendship with God because his righteous standard has been met. We have now been invited into a life of forgiveness. One of our goals is to keep short accounts with our shortcomings and the poor behavior of others. Colossians 3:13 raises the bar when it says, "Bear with each other and forgive one another if any of you has a grievance against someone. Forgive as the Lord forgave you." In other words, we are called to forgive everybody for everything. The best way I know of to keep short accounts is to follow this simple process each day:

- Pray this prayer, *Dear Jesus, please bring to my mind anyone I need to forgive that I am ready to deal with today*. Don't try to come up with people or situations. Just repeat these words sincerely.
- Write down any situations that come to mind. You don't need to describe the situation in detail. You just need simple notes as reminders.
- Walk each situation through the following six statements out loud.

The Six Statements of Forgiveness

1. I forgive (name the person) for (name the offense) (Colossians 3:13).
2. I admit that what happened was wrong (Romans 3:23).
3. I do not expect this person to make up for what they have done (2 Corinthians 5:17).
4. I will not use the offense to define who this person is (Ephesians 2:12-13).
5. I will not manipulate this person with this offense (Luke 6:37).
6. I will not allow what has happened to stop my personal growth (2 Peter 3:18).

If you are able to sincerely say all six statements in relation to a situation that is bothering you, you have forgiven. If you can't get through all six statements, don't be too hard on yourself. You are simply not ready. Ask God to prepare your heart to be able to forgive, and then try again tomorrow.

As you keep this process alive and active, God will faithfully lead you through any and all issues that need forgiveness in the order they are best worked on. He has the wisdom to know exactly how to lead you to a place of complete freedom from bitterness.

The Pursuit of Excellence

The power of grace does not end with forgiveness. It also becomes a strong motivation to live with excellence. This is what Paul was referring to when he wrote that grace "teaches us to say 'No' to ungodliness and worldly passions, and to live self-controlled, upright and godly lives in this present age" (Titus 2:11-12). Since you are forgiven, there is a sense in which everything in life is an option. There is no condemnation for those who are in Christ (Romans 8:1), so your relationship with God is not about forbidden things anymore. Instead, it is now a pursuit of living the best and healthiest life possible since you are free to do so.

Let me illustrate this. Imagine that four different beverages are set in front of you:

Beverage 1: A glass of ice water.

Beverage 2: An energy drink with bright packaging and dazzling promises.

Beverage 3: A can of your favorite soft drink.

Beverage 4: A mixture of vegetable juices including spinach, broccoli, brussels sprouts, carrots, and beets. Also included is a generous portion of tabasco sauce, soy sauce, garlic, castor oil, cinnamon, vinegar, mayonnaise, mustard, barbecue sauce, and lemon juice. To top it off just right, we add a ground-up jalapeño pepper and a handful of chocolate chips. We then puree it in a blender and make it available to you.

Scenario 1 (The Law)

What would your reaction be if I said to you, "You can choose whatever beverage you want except that you cannot have beverage 4. It is off limits because it is not good for you, so under no circumstance are you free to choose 4."

Some of you would say, "Okay, I don't want it anyway." Most of us, however, would be plagued with curiosity. We would begin to think, *Why can't I have that drink? I have never put those ingredients together, but maybe they are good together. Would it really be bad for me or is there some benefit I'm not aware of. Why should I take his word for it? I think I should test it for myself.* Intellectually, we know the fourth drink is not the best option, but because we dislike being told what to do, we become overly curious about it and maybe even inclined to crave it.

Scenario 2 (Grace)

What would your reaction be if I said to you, "You can choose whatever beverage you would like. No restrictions, no conditions, no demands. You are free to select the drink that is most appealing to you." Under these circumstances, you will naturally choose the beverage you consider to be the best option. If you don't choose the best one, others would wonder what is wrong with you. When given this kind of freedom, who *wouldn't* want the best?

In this same way, moral excellence goes hand in hand with grace. When there is no condemnation and an atmosphere of freedom, you will be naturally motivated to choose the path you determine to be the best course of action. You wouldn't drive a slow car when a fast car is freely available. You wouldn't choose moldy bread when fresh bread is accessible. You wouldn't choose to wear clothes that are ratty and too small when an attractive, well-fitting wardrobe was at your disposal. It just wouldn't make sense. Grace sets us free to apply this same kind of thinking to our moral lives.

The payoff is that moral excellence benefits everyone we love. Our wives develop a strong sense of trust when they are confident of our moral choices. Since trust is the key element in her life for making decisions, setting up budgets, raising children, and experiencing sexual satisfaction, moral excellence improves all the vital areas of your marriage.

Your kids naturally look up to you as a role model. They respect you and consider you to be one of the most important people in their lives. When your moral life is in order, that respect remains intact and their confidence in you operates at a very high level. Your advice is welcomed and your wisdom is readily accepted.

As you get older, people in your community will want you to have a significant and positive influence. They will value your wisdom, recognize your contribution, and long to hear from you as they work through decisions. Their belief that your moral life is following a path of excellence will heighten their confidence in you.

Skilled Lovers Are Curious

Everyone who is important to you is different from you. They have a collection of unique abilities that enables them to make a unique contribution to the world. Some of the skills they possess may be similar to yours, but the combination of traits is unique to them.

As a result, you can never fully understand the people you care about. There is always something new to learn about them. There is always something about them that is mysterious. They have within them the ability to surprise you regularly with new insight, new accomplishments, and new ideas.

Therefore, remaining curious about and interested in others is a key way to love them. As soon as you believe that you know everything there is to know about a person you value, the relationship begins to deteriorate. Nobody wants to be figured out, boxed in, and explained away as if they are finished products. They want to know they are fascinating enough to hold your attention.

So how do you cultivate curiosity in relationships?

Ask questions.

People long to know they have value. When you ask questions about areas of life they are interested in, you invest in them and emphasize their value. There are a variety of kinds of questions you can choose from.

Connection Questions

Everyone you know is emotionally attached to their lives. They love sports or clothes or friends or learning or technology. It is different with each person, but everyone loves something. When you show interest in these areas, you create an emotional environment that will draw the two of you together. At times this is easy because the person you are talking with loves the same things you love. At other times, this is a stretch because the people you love are very interested in things you don't care about.

For instance, my three sons all love sports. We can talk about competition, training, game strategy, and schedules with ease. We share a common love of these things so conversation picks up steam quickly. When I am with them, I ask questions about their achievements and I ask them to talk about their expertise in their fields.

My wife and daughters-in-law are a different story. They all love ministry and are all crazy about the grandkids, so when we are on these topics, it flows easily. They are also extremely interested in clothing, healthy food preparation, and the current events in their friends' relationships. I know these issues are important, but I lack the emotional attachment they have to such things. When it's time to engage on these topics, I have to make a deliberate choice to be curious. I ask them to describe how they make fashion choices, what their favorite shopping experiences have been, what it's like to figure out outfits and menus. When I'm brave, I even ask them how they keep track of so many details in people's lives, and then I listen as long as I can.

Emotional Questions

Everyone you know is going to experience setbacks and heartaches. If you've been good at asking emotional questions, it is likely they will want to talk with you when they experience hurt and disappointment. Your curiosity will help them heal even if you have no idea what advice to give them. This list of questions can help guide you.

- How did it make you feel when this happened?
- If you could say something to the other person right now, what would you say?
- Have you thought about what your plan is from here?
- What advice would you give to someone who just went through what you experienced?

Timing is important on these questions. If they don't elicit a response (or a reaction), just let it go. If the questions give the other person permission to talk and they discuss more than you expected, don't interrupt. This is not the time for problem solving. You are simply helping your loved one grieve, process, or evaluate their experience by providing a safe environment to release emotional pain through conversation.

Informational Questions

Anytime you can legitimately ask someone you love to give you advice, you raise their sense of value. My wife is remarkable at networking. My oldest son loves worship music. My oldest daughter-in-law can find a deal with great skill. My middle son can diagnose physical obstacles to working out as well as anyone I know. His wife knows how to build friendships that stick. My youngest son is great at diagnosing mechanical issues with cars and other machines. When I need advice in these areas, I make it a point to ask them. A lot of it I could figure out on my own, but I ask them because it enhances our relationship while leading to solutions.

Speak Love with Your Body

Your body speaks long before you utter a word. Your body language is so powerful it can completely override the words you use. If others are paying attention, they can tell a lot about you and your thoughts by observing your body language:

- They can tell if you are angry.
- They can predict the emotions in your heart.
- They can tell if you trying to intimidate them.
- They can tell when you are sad.
- They can tell when you have had a significant spiritual experience.

- They can tell you are sincere.
- They can tell if you respect them.
- They can tell when your heart is filled with joy.
- They can tell if there is romantic attraction.

Unfortunately, most of us give little thought to our body language. We assume our words are sufficient as we fail to realize how much nonverbal communication either adds to or detracts from the message we are trying to deliver. Most men don't spend time thinking about this so we default to doing what we grew up around. If our parents were skilled at nonverbal communication, we pick it up by example. If our parents were unskilled, we simply do the same thing and wonder why so many of our attempts to relate to other people don't turn out the way we planned.

Let Your Body Talk

Effective nonverbal communication is a skill that can be learned. Here are a few clear guidelines that will help you utilize body language in your favor.

Adjust body motions to the size of your audience. The smaller your audience, the smaller your body motions should be. If you are engaged in a private conversation, keep your hands closer to your body and use smaller gestures. Large motions in close proximity either express insecurity on your part or appear to be an attempt to intimidate the person you are talking with.

Lean toward the other person. Leaning forward expresses interest in what the other has to say. If you lean too far forward, it appears you are too eager or trying to take over. Slouching back in a chair or on the couch screams that you are not really interested and are just putting in time because you know you are supposed to. Instead, when someone wants to speak with you, it is key to put down what is in your hands, look away from the computer screen, or refocus faraway thoughts and turn your chair toward the person and say, "I am listening. I want to hear what you have to say." Even without the words, your action has expressed this sentiment.

Keep your posture open. Sitting with your arms and legs crossed gives the impression you are not really interested in anything that might be said. It appears you would rather be anywhere else, doing anything else rather than having this conversation. If, on the other hand, your hands are resting on your legs and both your legs are parallel to the floor, you will give an unmistakable message of interest.

Establish connection with gentle, respectful physical contact. Conversations that begin with a quick hug, handshake, or high five tend to start better and are more relaxed. Our bodies are wired to release endorphins into the blood system when we are affectionate with another human being. The result is a lower heart rate, lower blood pressure, relaxed muscles, and a general sense of well-being. This is why we often recoil from loved ones when we are not ready to be touched. It isn't that we don't want to be touched. It is just that it has such a powerful impact on us.

Make eye contact. You look at people you are interested in because it conveys sincerity. Your eyes, more than any other part of your body, express what is really going on in your heart. When you are ashamed, you avoid eye contact. When you are embarrassed, you avoid eye contact. When you are upset, you avoid eye contact. On the other hand, you will make eye contact when there is trust, appreciation, or fascination.

Keeping eye contact is not the same as staring. A focus that is too intense makes people feel like you are interrogating rather than relating to them. A good rule of thumb is the few-second rule. Make eye contact for two to ten seconds at a time. Casually look away and then reengage for another two to ten seconds. When you become comfortable with this process, you will express to others a genuine interest in what they have to say even if they can't figure out why.

Body language is a powerful form of communication, and it is worth working on in every arena of life. But we can easily become self-absorbed, stressed, or lazy and just slack off using the body language that says, "You are valuable. You are worth my time and energy." Strategic body language says all that before a word is ever spoken.

Define Your Relationships

Relationships in your life can range from casual to intense. As a result, healthy relationships are those that are defined, and unhealthy relationships are undefined and out of control. When you take time to define the relationships in your life, you are better able to figure out how to interact with the people you care about most and those you are just getting to know. For reference, consider the following relationship hierarchy:

Relationship Hierarchy

Level of Involvement	**Type of Relationship**		
	Friendships	***Work Relationships***	***Family Relationships***
Cautious	Acquaintances	Acquaintances	Distant relatives
Curious	Casual friends/ Romantic interests	Colleagues	Relatives you spend casual time with
Confident	Trusted friends/ Exclusive dating	Trainees	Influential relatives
Connected	Mentors	Mentors	Fiancée
Committed			Spouse/Children

Cautious Relationships

When engaging with people you either don't know very well or you know are not trustworthy, it is wise to act with caution. Limit the amount of time you spend with them, only share information you would be willing to post in public spaces, and politely disregard advice they volunteer. It is fine to talk about vacations, hobbies, and tasks at work, but you will not want to divulge your dreams, fears, or disappointments. And you definitely will not want to share any of those details about those you care about, especially your family. If you share vulnerable truths about yourself with acquaintances, you will attract unhealthy people to yourself and be consistently disappointed by the friends you keep.

All relationships start at this level. When you meet someone new, you may be meeting a great friend, a mentor, or someone who should never be more than just an acquaintance. You can't tell at first if this person is weird or wonderful. It is helpful, therefore, to learn to ask simple questions about people who are new in your life. You can actually ask the same questions of everyone you meet. As they talk about themselves, you will form an initial impression of how healthy this person is. If you determine they would be a distraction in your life, you can keep the conversation very simple and severely limit future contact. If, however, your first impression is positive, you can continue the conversation and look for other opportunities to interact. As you think about meeting new people, decide ahead of time that you will ask these questions:

5 Questions to Ask in the First 5 Minutes

1. What is your name?
2. How long have you been a part of this organization? church? group? (Never ask, "Are you new here?" If they are new, they already feel awkward about it. If they aren't, you will look stupid.)

3. Where do you work or go to school?
4. Who are the members of your family?
5. Where did you grow up?

Curious Relationships

Some of your acquaintances will progress to become friends, casual dating relationships (if you are single), and colleagues. These are still casual relationships, but you have determined you have enough in common that it is worth investigating. You still don't know how much you can trust them with, but you like spending time with them. You make progress in these relationships by remaining curious and sharing your preferences with one another in music, entertainment, and free-time activities.

If the friendship continues to grow, you will want to add in discussions about personal growth preferences and simple problem-solving situations. You still want to be cautious at this point because not all casual friends prove to be faithful and trustworthy. You don't want to open up yet about your hurts and fears or your most important dreams. Most of your casual friends will remain casual and cannot handle intimate knowledge about your past or your dreams. Be content to keep it casual and have fun with these people.

Confident Relationships

The folks who gain your confidence earn enough trust that you can share significant truths about your life with them. They are your trusted friends, close relatives, and exclusive dating interests (if single). These also include people you train at work. The work relationships are more limited, but you have enough confidence in them that you're willing to invest time in them. These people rise to this level because they have proved themselves to be emotionally safe and socially enjoyable.

Chances are, these people share your convictions and respect your privacy. You can, therefore, explore more sensitive information. You can share your dreams and the obstacles you have overcome. You can share the most significant steps of growth you have taken and the plans you intend to pursue next. You can also share from your areas of expertise with freedom and enthusiasm since these people respect you and want to learn from you.

Connected Relationships

Along your journey, you are going to encounter a few people who qualify to be truly connected with you. The most common are mentors. These are people who have developed abilities that you desire and the character to be trusted with your training and desire to grow. These have proven to be trustworthy at the deepest levels. As a result, they are very influential in helping you become a better person. They may be specific mentors who help you get better in a particular area or they may be general mentors you want to learn from in multiple areas.

You may also discover someone you will consider spending the rest of your life with. As you date seriously and move toward engagement, you will want to weigh the emotional and spiritual potential of the relationship by sharing the deep things of your life to ensure you can trust this person with the stuff that most people don't know. The agonizingly slow areas of growth, the hurts from your past, and the disappointments that have left you scarred need to be shared to give you the confidence that you can live with each other for the rest of your lives. You can hide these things from those who don't live in your home. but they will be exposed when you share the same address.

Committed Relationships

One type of relationship stands apart from all the others and we call it marriage. It requires special skills, exclusive focus, and a rock-solid commitment. Once you get married, the goal of this relationship becomes different from all other relationships. As a husband, the goal that makes marriage work is the pursuit to reach your wife's heart as often as possible. Everything in her life is connected emotionally, so anything you do to touch her heart makes her more confident, more interested in you, and easier to live with. So, if you want to be a skilled lover whose wife likes to meet you in the bedroom often, practice these simple skills. They might seem unrelated, but they are at the heart of how your wife pictures love and responds to love.

Compliment Her Often

The Gottman Institute has established that healthy marriages engage in five positive interactions for every negative one.[11] This is primarily because every sincere compliment your wife receives from you knits her heart to you, convinces her she is safe with you, and makes her feel like she is making life better for you and everyone in her family. These are powerful forces that soften her heart and make you more attractive to her. As men, we get tired of lavishing attention on our wives because it seems trivial to us after a while. In reality, it is one of the keys to being a skilled lover.

Help Her with Responsibilities

Women have an insatiable desire to make life better for the people they love. As a result, they tend to overcommit themselves with tasks designed to make their loved ones feel important. Anyone who "comes to her rescue" earns a special place in her heart. Every act of kindness raises her confidence that she can actually make things better, and even if she falls short, you are there to fill in. It still sounds strange to me when Pam tells other people that it is sexy when I vacuum or help with the dishes. Sexy, in my mind, includes lingerie, candles, and singular focus. In her mind, it includes every nice thing I've said and done during the past week.

Date Her

When you set time aside to spend time with her, she senses her value. When you plan topics beyond bills, tasks to be finished, and issues with the kids, you ignite once again the spark that first drew her to you and you to her. Very few men can spontaneously come up with sensitive, emotionally based topics to discuss. It is strategic, therefore, to preplan the opening question on your dates to get the conversation moving in a sensitive, romantic direction. Some of my favorite questions are:

- "If you had an unlimited budget, what is the one thing you would most like to do in your life?"
- "How would you describe the dream in your heart? What about its fulfillment would make your life feel complete?"
- "If you described yourself as a vehicle, which one would it be? If you described me as a vehicle, which one would it be?"
- "What is your favorite movie?" (Extra points if you watch it together—probably with Kleenex.)
- "What is your favorite vacation ever?"
- "What is your favorite childhood memory?"
- "What is your favorite memory with our kids?"

You can find other questions in relationship books and on various websites or you can ask your friends what has worked for them.

The key is to get in the habit of using intimate, relational questions to keep your hearts connected along your journey. Most of these questions you probably wouldn't ask your best friends, but they will help you reach your wife's heart.

Helping Kids with Choices

The other uniquely committed relationships of your life are with your kids. Being a skilled lover of your kids means harnessing the decisive influence God has entrusted you with. Ephesians 6:4 says, "Fathers, do not exasperate your children; instead, bring them up in the training and instruction of the Lord."

The first step of loving your kids is to realize that you have the potential to exasperate your kids or make them angry. A dad who is never pleased with his kids, criticizes everything they do, and demands that they always produce more and act better will watch them diminish in motivation and accomplishments.

The way to combat this is to focus on "training" and "instruction." "Training" refers to discipline that leads to self-discipline. The first goal of fatherhood is to raise young people who have the ability to discipline their time, their desires, their habits, and their commitments. Early in their lives, we apply discipline and make many decisions for them. As soon as they are ready, the goal elevates to challenging them to make decisions based on wisdom and an understanding of natural consequences.

"Instruction" is not the average word for teaching. It refers to an admonition to do the right thing. The second goal of fatherhood is an appeal to kids to do what is right because it is the right thing to do. It includes an appeal to spiritual integrity, moral excellence, relational respect, and personal growth. In short, we are trying to get young people to make good decisions.

To assist us in the process, I describe in *The 10 Best Decisions a Man Can Make* some tests we can apply to any decision to help us be more skilled. Here's a summary of these tests:

Decision-Making Test 1: The Obvious Test

When you are faced with a decision, it's helpful to determine if this is a simple decision or a more complicated one. As a result, before you put a lot of effort into any decision, ask yourself, "Is this decision so obvious that I'm wasting time thinking about it?"

Decision-Making Test 2: The Wisdom Test

The Wisdom Test is a set of questions you ask when faced with a decision that is not immediately obvious. If you answer yes to all these questions, it is pretty clear that your decision is based on wisdom and you probably ought to proceed forward. If you answer no to all these questions, your course of action will become equally obvious. If you have a balanced mixture of yes and no, there is more rigorous work to do to figure out the best course of action.

- Does this decision line up with my convictions?
- Will the people I respect most agree with this decision?
- Have I asked them?
- Is this decision based on healthy boundaries that will produce self-respect?
- Will this decision cause personal growth in my life?
- Will this decision improve my most important relationships?
- Would I encourage my best friends to make this same decision?

Decision-Making Test 3: The Priority Test

Step 1: Write out your decision in a positive way. Describe the decision before you in terms of what you will do if you say yes to this decision. For instance, "I am considering moving my family to Colorado to begin working for a company there that would result in a pay increase." This is better than "I am considering turning down the job offer in Colorado" because it encourages you to think about momentum in your life. Whichever way you go with a decision like this, you will define the direction you are going to take. Either way is a victory because you will take full ownership of your choice and put your heart into it. You don't want to leave room for negative thinking.

Step 2: Make a Pro/Con list.

- Create two columns on a sheet of paper.
- On one side write down the reasons why you *ought* to take this course of action.
- On the other side write down the reasons why this course of action is *not* a good idea.

Step 3: Prioritize the reasons. In both columns, prioritize the reasons you have listed. It has been my experience that most people are better with an *A, B, C* system. This means you assign an *A* to the vital reasons you identify. The supportive reasons will get a *B*. And *C* is reserved for the reasons you came up with because you are creative and can come up with ideas that don't really impact the decision.

Step 4: Compare the high priority reasons from both lists. Evaluate the *A* reasons for saying yes with the *A* reasons for choosing no. If it is a tie, then move to the *B* reasons to see if the decision becomes clear. Don't be fooled by volume. It is quite possible that one list will have more reasons than the other, but this is inconsequential. Volume is no substitute for quality, and decisions such as this require high-quality conclusions. The way to build clarity is to deliberately prioritize the evidence and discipline yourself to focus on the *A* reasons.

All of us evaluate the quality of our lives based on the state of our important relationships. "And so we know and rely on the love

God has for us. God is love. Whoever lives in love lives in God, and God in them" (1 John 4:16).

Fun Thoughts on the Power of Love

> Q: How can a stranger tell if two people are married?
>
> A: You might have to guess, based on whether they seem to be yelling at the same kids. (Derrick, age 8)
>
> Q: How do you decide who to marry?
>
> A: You got to find somebody who likes the same stuff. If you like sports, she should like it that you like sports, and she should keep the chips and dip coming. (Alan, age 10)
>
> Q: When is it okay to kiss someone?
>
> A: When they're rich. (Pam, age 7)
>
> Q: How would you make a marriage work?
>
> A: Tell your wife that she looks pretty, even if she looks like a truck. (Ricky, age 10)[12]

CHAPTER 7

Finish What You Start

A man who waits for rewards can accomplish anything.

If your mind isn't clouded
by unnecessary things,
this is the best season of your life.

Wu-Men

The year was 2003. San Marcos High School was playing Brawley High School on a hot, humid night in the Imperial Valley of California. My son Zachery was on the SMHS team, and much to my delight, he scored two touchdowns in the first half. After the first three quarters, San Marcos had a commanding fourteen-point lead.

It would have been a spectacular night except there was a fourth quarter. Our young men weren't prepared for the humidity. Exhaustion took over. The once stubborn defense lost the ability to tackle. Superior speed turned into lethargic chasing. Hustling athletes were reduced to huffing and puffing spectators. Brawley scored three times in the final period to win the game. Many of the San Marcos players, including our son, had to drink Pedialyte (a product that helps prevent dehydration) just to gain enough energy to get on the bus for a long ride home.

They started spectacularly. They put on a dominant performance and performed like champions for three quarters of the game. The only problem is they didn't finish well.

For Zach and his teammates, it was one football game from

which they could recover quickly and move on with their lives. At the same time, it was a lesson for them about life. Victory comes at the end of our ventures. That is why men finish what they start.

Men Finish Projects

Throughout history, men have worked on projects. Noah was called into service because he "found favor in the eyes of the LORD" (Genesis 6:8). It is common to view long-term, strenuous, and difficult projects as punishment rather than statements of approval. In Noah's case, God have him the hardest job on earth because he was pleased with him. The task was characterized by hardships:

- The project probably took somewhere between forty and seventy-five years to complete.[13]
- All his neighbors were hostile or indifferent, in denial (Genesis 6:11; Matthew 24:37-39).
- Nothing like an ark had ever existed, so Noah had nothing to base his plans on other than the specifications God gave him (Genesis 6:14-16).
- Noah sounded ridiculous when he warned the people of a coming deluge. It's even possible that nothing like rain had ever been heard of (Genesis 2:5-6).
- He worked with the understanding that the end of his project would usher in the destruction of all other people.

It would have been easy to give in to the criticism and give up. He was, however, determined to finish the project God had assigned to him.

It is common for men to lose interest during the last stages of any project. The thrill of something new has long evaporated. Their enthusiasm about the project has been replaced with comments such as, "How long is this going to take? Will this ever be done? Has this project become more important than us?"

As a result, a man's character is revealed at the end of a project rather than at the beginning. A man's willingness to jump into a project demonstrates that he is brave and willing to risk. His determination to finish the venture reveals whether he is run by his whims or by his character.

Finish Your Marriage

Marriage was first defined in Genesis 2:24, "That is why a man leaves his father and mother and is united to his wife, and they become one flesh." This idea has evolved into public celebrations in which we proclaim in the presence of God and others, "I promise to keep only to you as long as we both shall live." We live in a world, however, that does not view these words as binding. They have become a traditional reference in the ceremony that is more like decoration than a declaration.

It has become a countercultural trait to champion lifelong marriage and to tenaciously hold to your commitment to love and cherish the same woman all the days of your life. I can guarantee that you are going to be unhappy with the wife of your youth at various times in your life together. She will be controlling, unreasonable, manipulative, and critical at times. But she will also walk alongside you as the most supportive, loving, and encouraging person in your life at other times. If you want to find reasons for giving up on this most intimate and complex of human relationships, they won't be difficult to come up with.

What would this say about you, however? I am not naïve about the difficulties that exist in marriage. I hear the stories every week, and I have spent the last thirty years helping people hold their relationships together amidst unimaginable and intense conflicts. I am painfully aware of how contentious marriage relationships can become. I have witnessed people blow up their marriages over money, sexual dissatisfaction, extramarital affairs, perceived lack of support, anger, racial tensions, family attachments, and boredom. The list is endless.

At the same time, every intimate relationship is one breakthrough away from reestablishing trust and rediscovering the love that brought you together in the first place. A man who is committed to finish what he started will tenaciously seek after that breakthrough with hopeful patience. A man who is not committed to finish will drop out of the race when it becomes more inconvenient than his expectations allow.

Don't overreact if you happen to be on a second or third marriage. God's grace is big enough to handle the complications and challenges that have become your reality. It is time, however, for you to say, "I have made mistakes in the past, but from this day forward, I will finish what I started with my wife. We will outlast our disagreements, work through our conflicts, invest in our love for each other, and work together to build a life that will leave a godly legacy. There will be no more giving up on the commitment I have made."

Many of the men I meet are either overwhelmed or confused in their marriage relationships. Women build trust, approach the importance of interaction, and respond to stress different from men. This creates a constant source of surprise and confusion for men as we were hoping we were marrying a "buddy" who was way better looking than our male friends.

It is impossible to boil down all the nuances of a lifelong marriage relationship in a few simple habits, but most of us simply need a working knowledge. We don't understand the details of our computers or the detailed operation of our vehicles. We do know how to drive our cars and operate our computers and that allows us to enjoy the great value they bring to our lives. In the same way, you don't need to know the intricacies of how your wife operates. Instead, you need a true, working knowledge of how to relate to her.

Becoming skilled at the following simple measures will make an intimate relationship with your wife work and will help you be a man who finishes what he starts.

Keep a Good Sense of Humor

Nobody has a perfect relationship, so a good sense of humor helps relationships stick. Take your wedding vows seriously, but don't take yourselves too seriously. Ask yourself if you can relate to this story.

> A solicitor for the Red Cross called upon a well-to-do young couple for a donation. Hearing a commotion inside he knocked extra-loudly on the door. A somewhat disheveled man admitted him in. "What can I do for you?" he growled, clearly upset about something. "I would like to speak to the master of the house," said the solicitor politely. "Then you're just in time," barked the young man. "My wife and I are settling that very question right now!"[14]

Monitor Her Security

The emotional need your wife feels most often is an intense desire for security. It determines the quality of everything in her life and governs her stress level. Simply put, it is a foreign language for us men. We know security is an issue, but it is not in our top five. You will seldom, if ever, hear a man ask a friend, "Are you feeling safe today?" We see no point in the question because it is overshadowed by the more important questions of competence, confidence, and competition. For the woman you married, the safety question is an all-consuming pursuit. For her needs, security includes:

- physical safety
- having enough money to meet the needs of her family
- being valued by the people she loves the most

- having opportunities to express herself and her convictions
- having opportunities to be productive
- having a place to call home
- having time to take care of herself
- being pampered every once in a while
- knowing that her husband cares about the things that are important to her
- the freedom to be who she is today

Without a doubt, the last statement, "the freedom to be who she is today," is at the heart of what it means to be secure. Her life is constantly changing. It begins with the "gift" of menstruation. This lovely part of her life guarantees that her emotions, her body, and her outlook on life are in constant motion. Some days, she feels great about herself, making her a joy to live with. On other days, she feels bloated, ugly, and worthless, which deflates the joy out of your day like a flat tire. Still other days find her sad, anxious, and overreactive. And these days come and go every month. As a result, she is very interesting to live with!

I have been married now for more than thirty years, and I would love to tell you I totally understand my wife's need for security. That would be like saying I know what it's like to give birth to a baby. As men, we will never fully understand our wives, but we can learn how to address this most important of her needs with a few simple skills.

Turn Off the Problem Solver

Our default position is to be a problem solver. When our wives want to talk, we assume there is a problem to solve. We long to be heroic for her by coming up with a solution that will dazzle her.

The problem is that it makes her feel inadequate or inferior when you think she needs to have her problems solved for her.

Make Sandwiches Often

Begin and end most of your conversations with compliments, like bread on a sandwich. Rather than saying, "I already knew that," say, "It is remarkable that you care about our family so much. I was already aware of that information, but I think it's awesome that you wanted me to be filled in. And besides, you are so cute when you express yourself with such intensity."

I know this sounds like you are overdoing it. I also know that many of you are thinking this is coddling her with undue sensitivity. If she were a man, I would agree with you. This is one of those areas where we need to man up and treat her like a woman.

View Interaction as Recreation

I was having an honest conversation with my wife recently about a man's sex drive. I described to her it was like a powerful sports car with a big engine. A man who accepts this will treat his sexual interest with respect and will guard it. I asked her, "What is the equivalent to this in a woman's life?" Her response was, "Clothes and relationships. Women dream about clothes, and every outfit changes her confidence level and emotional well-being. Relationships are even bigger. In fact, relationships are like jet fuel to women."

This creates a huge challenge for us. We tend to think all conversations have a main point. We look for the point and feel successful when we find it. Our wives, on the other hand, often engage in conversation as if it's a recreational activity. It is similar to hiking, playing a basketball game, going hunting, or attending a sporting event.

The only point for her is to have fun and connect with others. Those who willingly connect with her and take the journey with her become trusted individuals in her heart. Husbands who resist or act like all of this is strange will make their wife wonder if they are interested enough in her to be trustworthy.

The challenge exists because we don't interact this way. I would never look you in the eyes and say, "I want to hear all about your week. Please tell me every detail." You would wonder what is wrong with me and what agenda I was pushing. Rather than believe I am truly interested, you would be suspicious of me. As a result, the only place we can work on this skill is in the context of our marriage, and we will do that only if we value this need in our wife's life.

Be Her Best Friend

Studies have demonstrated that one of the most important contributors to a successful marriage is the friendship between a man and his wife.[15] As responsibility grows, romantic attraction needs the push of friendship to overcome the interruptions of life. Simple steps you can take to be her best friend include:

Speak her love language. Gary Chapman wisely points out in *The Five Love Languages* how each of us receives love. The five languages are words of affirmation, gifts, physical touch, acts of service, and quality time. Practice approaching your wife with each of these five and take note of which one(s) she responds to most favorably. Then deliberately use that approach as often as possible.

Seek to lower her stress. Friends have a natural way of lowering stress in each other's lives. The acceptance and camaraderie of friendship raises confidence and makes life feel easier than it would be if faced alone. Ask your wife what tends to raise stress in her life and what you have done in the past that helps alleviate that stress. Then pray for wisdom to be someone in her life who lowers stress as much as possible.

Sincerely compliment her. Women tend to build confidence based on the opinion of the people they care about. When you point out her strengths, admire her beauty, appreciate her contribution to your life, and flirt with her, it triggers a response in her to feel better about herself and elevates her confidence.

Accept her slow-growth areas. You have become skilled at living with your talents and deficiencies because you don't have any other choice. You are aware that you have some unique abilities that are efficient and highly effective in producing results you enjoy. At the same time, in some areas of your life you are stubbornly immature. You overreact to certain situations and cannot give a good reason why. You have habits that improve only a little even when you put enormous amounts of focus and discipline into them. You have attitudes that are childish, and at times you engage in behaviors that you instruct other people to avoid.

Your wife is the same way. Some of her traits are awesome and impressive. Others are improving as slowly as certain areas of your life. Our tendency is to be critical and demanding in these areas rather than accepting and supportive.

Express loyalty. In John 15:13, Jesus told his followers, "Greater love has no one than this: to lay down one's life for one's friends." With your true friends, you do what it takes to defend their honor, help them succeed, and protect them from harm. In essence, you lay down your life for your friends.

Loyalty is a simple concept when you agree with everything your friend is doing. It's quite another thing when a friend embarrasses you, acts foolishly, or takes a stand you don't agree with. In addition, we live in a world that is critical, immoral, and self-absorbed, so your best friend will be criticized and mistreated. Loyalty will compel you to stand by her no matter what. Even when she is wrong or deserves the criticism, you will stand together because friendship is stronger than your imperfections.

Listen to her advice. "You are my friends if you do what I command," would have been a strange sounding challenge from Jesus to his disciples (John 15:14). This was their rabbi, their leader, their teacher, and the hope of their future. They were not used to thinking of the authority in their lives as a friend. Jesus, however, understood that a part of friendship is giving and receiving advice. Your friends observe you in many different settings. They see the best in you, the worst in you, and the mediocre in you.

There are times when your friends possess the perspective that you need. Healthy friends, therefore, accept advice from their friends when they are right. This is an especially difficult part of a marriage friendship. Your love gives you an intense level of influence in each other's lives. You can reach a place in each other's hearts that no one else can reach. As a result, your encouragement of one another is more motivating than encouragement from anyone else. Likewise, any criticism you share has the potential to hurt at a deeper level than criticism from anyone else.

Open doors of opportunity for her. When I see an opportunity that is good for one of my friends, I tell him. When I find a pursuit that is big enough for others to experience also, I tell my friends about it. When I know of a training conference that is high quality, I invite my friends to join me. I want my friends to know about anything that is helping me be a better person.

If you and your wife are friends, you will be committed to do this same thing for each other. Yet this appears to be a major difficulty for modern couples. It appears that many people get married based on what they can get from the other person. We don't want our spouses to be too busy because we want to dominate their free time. We don't want our spouses to be too ambitious or to have too many interests because we want them to respond to our needs whenever we want those needs met. As a result, we end up stifling the growth of the one we love the most rather than looking for ways to open doors of opportunity that help her develop her full potential.

Look for ways to play together. A big part of being friends is having fun together. That sounds simple enough. In marriage, however, it's more of a challenge because men and women approach friendship differently. When a woman builds a friendship with other women, she and her friends share their hopes, dreams, thoughts, and current experiences in a dynamic flow of ideas. They love to interact and talk about what is happening in their lives. Women rate their friendship high when it is rich with conversation, vibrant with emotion, and characterized by cooperation.

Men, on the other hand, build friendship based on activities. They hunt together, fish together, work on computers together, build things together, make music together. While they do things side by side, they build camaraderie. Men rate a friendship high when it is fun, makes them feel capable, and lowers their stress.

Laugh together. Laughter improves your *physical health* by relaxing your entire body and leaving your muscles relaxed for up to forty-five minutes after. It boosts your immune system as it decreases stress hormones while increasing immune cells and infection-fighting antibodies. It also triggers the release of endorphins and protects your heart through increased blood flow.[16] Laughter improves your *mental health* by combating emotions that intensify stress, helping you relax, recharge, and increase your energy level, and shifting your perspective away from negative conclusions.[17] Finally, laughter is good for your *social health* by triggering the release of oxytocin and reminding you not to take yourself so seriously.

Finish Being a Dad

The most influential person in our lives is our dad. We all long to hear that he is proud of us and glad to be involved in our lives. The same is true for our kids this very moment. The profound influence we have on our kids in undeniable.

Create an environment. As we learned earlier, when dads roughhouse with their kids, they help them develop the ability to self-regulate their emotions and to change activity level quickly. We wrestle with them, hug them, and play games with them. These activities give the unmistakable message that we notice them and are interested in them. It also ramps up their activity level and intensifies the emotional environment. When dad steps out of the room, both levels diminish quickly. This trains kids to respond appropriately to the changing nature of life without overreacting or underperforming.

Show and tell your kids that you love them. Young people who have concluded that Dad is proud of them are more confident, more relaxed in peer relationships, more focused on academic and career achievement, and demonstrate more respect for those in leadership.

Provide answers and guidance. Young people (especially teenagers) turn to their dads to learn how to make decisions. They love their mom's input also, but they lean on Dad to help them think through issues that require a long-term choice.

Set an example through behavior and faith. We all tend to treat others the way our dads treated us and the members of our family. And many of us think God is a lot like our dad. So your fathering matters a great deal as does your example of faith. How you value your kids will impact how your children respond to, treat, and respect others throughout their lifetime. And how they interpret God's demeanor and love will be greatly influenced by how you have acted toward and loved them.

These are all commonly understood influences of a father on his family. It makes sense, therefore, for us to do our best and to determine in our hearts that we will be present and persistent in our efforts.

The following chart was very helpful to me as I tried to figure out how to be a dad. It is based on the idea that our kids will go through five stages in their development. During each of these stages, our kids experience unique needs and benefit from a certain approach to parenting.

Stage of Development	Approach to Life	Developmental Need	Parenting Approach
Early Childhood (birth to beginning of school)	**Dependency.** Kids are not able to take care of themselves and must depend on others for provisions and decision making.	**Bonding.** Kids learn their default relationship style, discover their importance to others, and discern safe people.	**Decision Maker.** Kids need someone to tell them what to do and discipline their behavior.
Childhood (beginning of school to puberty)	**Exploration.** Kids begin to realize life is big and filled with opportunity. This is a time to try out many things to determine aptitudes that are worth pursuing.	**Goal-Setting.** Kids need to determine what they are good at so they can use their strengths to develop a place of confidence in preparation for puberty.	**Director.** Kids need some freedom to explore but also need involved parents who set boundaries for their activities and friendships to maintain safety.
Adolescence (onset of puberty to beginning of college or career)	**Experimentation.** Teens experience intense physical development. In the process, their growth is driven by emotions more than thoughts. As a result, they experiment with different identities through social interactions to see which feels best to them.	**Decisions, Wisdom.** The guiding principle is "emotions follow decisions." Since adolescence is highly emotional, the better they become at decisions, the less emotional turmoil they experience.	**Coach.** Teens need to be challenged to make decisions while parents keep veto power. Useful tools include, "Tell me why I should say yes." "What discipline can I enact that will help soften your heart and convince you not to do this again?"

Stage of Development	Approach to Life	Developmental Need	Parenting Approach
Early Adulthood (beginning of career to maturity in their aptitudes)	**Application**. In adolescence, our sons and daughters make conclusions about who they are. It is now time to act on these conclusions to see if they work out.	**Mentor, Encourager**. It is vital that young adults take responsibility for their lives, but they long to hear from others who believe in them and are available to mentor them.	**Consultant**. Consultants wait to be asked. We can tell them, "If you ever have questions you would like to ask, I will do my best to answer them," and then pray they ask.
Adulthood	**Interdependence**. Adults realize they are talented and surrounded by equally talented people. As we work together, we accomplish more.	**Peer Relationship**. This is where we get to be friends with our kids.	**Peer**. When you recognize that your son or daughter is better than you at something and ask for their assistance, you elevate them to a place of being your peer.

Finish Your Legacy

You were created to build a legacy. It is in God's design for manhood. As he delivered the Ten Commandments, he included these words, "You shall not bow down to [an image] or worship them; for I, the Lord your God, am a jealous God, punishing the children for the sin of the parents to the third and fourth generation of those who hate me" (Exodus 20:5). Notice that a man's influence goes three or four generations deep. Verse 5 is the negative side of the formula, but the next verse points out that our positive influence is even more powerful: "But showing love to a thousand generations of those who love me and keep my commandments."

The point is inescapable. You were put on earth to influence generations of people who have yet to be born. You live in a world, however, that fights against this thinking. We are encouraged to be self-absorbed, self-centered, and focused on self-gratification. I took a look at current advertisements for examples of buying into a self-absorbed approach to life. Some of them included:

An ad for online greeting cards: "I don't care what you think of me. Unless you think I am awesome. In which case, you are right."[18]

An ad for gum: "A little piece of happy."

A soft drink ad: "Open happiness."

An ad for Sea-Monkeys: "Own a bowlful of happiness."

Automobile ad: "It's as wild as you want it to be."

Automobile ad: "Amazing from every point of view."

Automobile ad: "What's in it for you?"

Automobile ad: "Like a spirited woman who yearns to be tamed."

Ad for an edible arrangement: "When words fail, send something better."

There's nothing wrong, of course, with gum, greeting cards, fruit, and automobiles, but they can't bring lasting happiness and they certainly can't take the place of a legacy that helps your grandchildren and great-grandchildren live better lives.

Building a legacy is one of God's primary goals for us. Our days on earth are the preparation phase for our "real" life in eternity. Those who try to live just for today find they are never quite satisfied. Those who invest in their legacy experience a growing sense of dignity. Paul seeks to instill this kind of thinking into all believers in Colossians 3:2-4, "Set your minds on things above, not on earthly things. For you died, and your life is now hidden with Christ in God. When Christ, who is your life, appears, then you also will appear with him in glory."

There are some simple skills you can practice that will help you pass on what is important to you to future generations.

Your Biblical Legacy

Choose a few Bible verses that represent what is most important to you. Paste them into a file on your computer. Print these verses and post them somewhere in your house. At some point in your life, give a copy of these verses to everyone who is important to you. Some of my favorites are:

> Being confident of this, that he who began a good work in you will carry it on to completion until the day of Christ Jesus (Philippians 1:6).
>
> But whatever were gains to me I now consider loss for the sake of Christ. What is more, I consider everything a loss because of the surpassing worth of knowing Christ Jesus my Lord (Philippians 3:7-8).
>
> And the things you have heard me say in the presence of many witnesses entrust to reliable people who will also be qualified to teach others (2 Timothy 2:2).
>
> For in him all things were created: things in heaven and on earth, visible and invisible, whether thrones or powers or rulers or authorities; all things have been created through him and for him. He is before all things, and in him all things hold together (Colossians 1:16-17).
>
> No, in all these things we are more than conquerors through him who loved us. For I am convinced that neither death nor life, neither angels nor demons, neither the present nor the future, nor any powers, neither height nor depth, nor anything else in all creation, will be able to separate us from the love of God that is in Christ Jesus our Lord (Romans 8:37-39).

Trust in the LORD and do good;
dwell in the land and enjoy safe pasture.
Take delight in the LORD,
and he will give you the desires of your heart.
(Psalm 37:3-4)

God is our refuge and strength,
an ever-present help in trouble...
He says, "Be still, and know that I am God;
I will be exalted among the nations,
I will be exalted in the earth."
(Psalm 46:1,10)

Your Inspirational Legacy

Choose a few quotes from bumper stickers, quotation websites, movies, speeches, and books that have affected your life. Do the same thing with these as you do with your favorite Bible verses. A few of my favorites are:

- Experience is what you get when you don't get what you want.
- Life is what happens to you while you are busy making other plans.
- Pray like it depends upon God. Work like it depends upon you.
- He is no fool who gives what he cannot keep to gain that which he cannot lose.
- Where there is light, there are bugs.
- Fear and faith are the same thing pointed in exactly the opposite direction.

Your Financial Legacy

Jesus said, "For where your treasure is, there your heart will be also" (Luke 12:34). You are emotionally attached to your finances. The members of your family are also attached to your money, so at a family level, you can direct the emotional focus of those you want to influence by strategically directing money to the causes you care about.

To establish a financial legacy, choose a cause you care about. It could be missions outreach, sponsoring children in a third-world country, supporting orphans, military families, or local programs to help the homeless. Don't worry about how much you have to invest; just make sure you care about it. Invest regularly what you can. Then set up a time each year to report to your family the investment you have made and how it has helped others. You could make it part of your Thanksgiving celebration or your Christmas gift-giving tradition. Or you could choose a day for a family dinner specifically to talk over how your family is helping others less fortunate than you.

Finishing Is a Decision

Michael Hargrove relates a story that captures the power of choice when it comes to finishing the most important pursuits of life. Michael was waiting to pick up a friend at the Portland, Oregon, airport. He watched as a man stopped next to him to greet his family. First, he motioned to his youngest son (maybe six years old). After they gave each other a long, loving hug, the father looked his son in the eyes and said, "It's so good to see you, son. I missed you so much!"

His son smiled somewhat shyly, averted his eyes, and replied softly, "Me too, Dad."

Then the man stood up, gazed in the eyes of his oldest son

(maybe nine or ten), and said, "You're already quite the young man. I love you very much, Zach!"

Next the man turned his attention to the eighteen-month-old little girl who was squirming excitedly in her mother's arms. The man said, "Hi, baby girl!" as he gently took her from her mother. He kissed her face all over, held her close to his chest, and rocked her from side to side. The little girl relaxed and laid her head on his shoulder.

After several moments, he handed his daughter to his oldest son and declared, "I've saved the best for last!" He then proceeded to give his wife a long, passionate kiss and then silently mouthed the words, "I love you so much!"

Michael asked the man, "Wow! How long have you two been married?"

"We've been together for fourteen years, married twelve of those," he said without breaking his gaze from his lovely wife.

"Well then, how long have you been away?"

The man turned to look at Michael and said, "Two whole days!"

In stunned amazement, Michael replied, "I hope my marriage is still that passionate after twelve years!"

The man suddenly stopped smiling. He looked Michael straight in the eye and said, "Don't hope, friend...decide!"[19]

Notes

1. Katy Finneran, "The Greatest Risks They Ever Took," *Forbes*, January 21, 2010, www.forbes.com/2010/01/20/greatest-risk-they-took-entrepreneurs-management-risk_3.html.
2. "Pandora Reports Record 3QFY14 Financial Results," November 21, 2013, http://investor.pandora.com/phoenix.zhtml?c=227956&p=irol-newsArticle&ID=1879209&highlight=.
3. Finneran, "Greatest Risks."
4. Katy Finneran, "In Pictures: The Greatest Risk They Ever Took," *Forbes*, January 21, 2010, www.forbes.com/2010/01/20/gucci-indy500-letterman-entreprenuer-management-risk-greatest_slide_23.html.
5. For more information about Brian Blomberg and the National Center for Fathering, check out their website at http://fathers.com.
6. "Hilarious Jokes from the Guys Who Make America Laugh," *Reader's Digest*, www.rd.com/slideshows/hilarious-jokes/#ixzz2oEACvKj8.
7. The story of the London Tower Bridge was compiled from "Tower Bridge Facts," *Primary Facts*, May 6, 2013, http://primaryfacts.com/1339/tower-bridge-facts/; "History of Tower Bridge," *Topsail*, http://topsailevents.co.uk/tower-bridge-opening-tower-bridge-and-bridge-lift-information/history-of-tower-bridge; and "Bridge History," *Tower Bridge Exhibition*, http://www.towerbridge.org.uk/TBE/EN/BridgeHistory/.
8. Cited by John Haines, "What Would I Do Without Modern Technology?," *In Search of Simplicity* (blog), January 20, 2011, http://insearchofsimplicity.com/tag/humorous-stories/.
9. http://data.worldbank.org/country/united-states.
10. "Life Expectancy Tables," Department of Health and Human Resources, 1996, www.efmoody.com/estate/lifeexpectancy.html.
11. Ellie Lisitsa, "The Positive Perspective: Dr. Gottman's Magic Ratio!," *Gottman Institute Relationship Blog*, December 3, 2012, www.gottmanblog.com/2012/12/the-positive-perspective-dr-gottmans.html.
12. "Kids' Opinions on Marriage, Dating, and Relationships," *Collection of Awesome*, September 2, 2012, http://collectionofawesome.com/2012/02/09/kids-opinions-on-marriage-dating-and-relationships/.
13. The biblical record does not tell us how long it took Noah and his sons to build the ark. For discussion about the time involved, check out www.answersingenesis.org/articles/2010/06/01/long-to-build-the-ark and www.scriptureoncreation.org/#/bible-question-answer/how-long-to-build-the-ark.
14. *Great Clean Jokes*, www.greatcleanjokes.com/jokes/marriage-humor/relationship-jokes/.
15. Karen Peterson, "Friendship Makes Marriages a Success," *USA Today*, April 1, 1999, cited in http://lists101.his.com/pipermail/smartmarriages/1999-April/002094.html.

16. Adapted from "Laughter Is the Best Medicine," Helpguide.org, www.helpguide.org/life/humor_laughter_health.htm.

17. Ibid.

18. http://pandce.proboards.com/thread/10641.

19. Adapted from Michael D. Hargrove and Bottom Line Underwriters, Inc., "Don't Hope...Decide!" *Moral Stories*, September 26, 2008, http://academictips.org/blogs/dont-hopedecide/.

ABOUT THE AUTHOR

Bill Farrel has been impacting men's lives for twenty-five years as a senior pastor, youth pastor, radio talk-show host, community leader, and sought-after conference speaker. Bill has a unique ability to make biblical principles simple and practical so the average man knows how to live them out in his daily life.

Bill and his wife, Pam, are relationship specialists who help people discover how to be "Love-Wise." They are international speakers and authors of over thirty-five books, including the best-selling *Men Are Like Waffles—Women Are Like Spaghetti*. A few of their other books include *Red-Hot Monogamy*, *The 10 Best Decisions a Leader Can Make*, *The 10 Best Decisions a Man Can Make*, and *The 10 Best Decisions a Parent Can Make.*

Bill and Pam are frequent guests on radio and television, and their writing has appeared in numerous magazines and newspapers. Their books have been translated into more than sixteen languages. They have been happily married for over thirty years and are parents to three children, two daughters-in-law, two granddaughters, and one grandson. The Farrels live in San Diego, California.

To contact the Farrels or learn more about their other resources:

Love-Wise
3755 Avocado Boulevard, #414
La Mesa, CA 91941
(619) 328-0564
www.Love-Wise.com
info@Love-Wise.com
Like Bill and Pam Farrel on Facebook
Follow Bill Farrel or Pam Farrel on Twitter

To learn more about Harvest House books and to read sample chapters, visit our website:

www.harvesthousepublishers.com